FAMILY COUNSELING

A SYSTEMS APPROACH

Laura Sue Dodson, MSW, Ph.D.
Consultant in Family Therapy
Therapist in Private Practice
Denver, Colorado

In Collaboration With

DeWayne J. Kurpuis, Ed.D.
School of Education
Indiana University
Bloomington, Indiana

FOREWORD by Virginia Satir

Accelerated Development Inc.
2515 West Jackson
P. O. Box 667
Muncie, IN 47305

Library of Congress Catalog Card Number: 76-46908

International Standard Book Number: 0-915202-08-5

Corporate Editor: Linda K. Davis

Corporate Illustrator: Mary J. Blizzard

Printed in the United States of America

Order additional copies from

 Accelerated Development Inc.
Publication Division
P. O. Box 667
Muncie, Indiana 47305

Cost $7.95 plus postage and handling
              in U. S. and Canada add 50 cents
              in other countries, postage depends upon
                  prevailing rates

Price is subject to change without notice

To

Hal, Mimi, and George

who have been my most intimate
fellow journeyers
and teachers.

FOREWORD

This book is really about music, human music as played by
human beings as they struggle to live together in their family
--inharmonious and unpleasant when things are going badly,
and harmonious and pleasant when things are going well. I
am likening the family to a mini-orchestra, for I see many
parallels.

Laura Dodson, as the orchestra leader (family counselor),
tells us how she orchestrates new music, with the intent that
the family will reach the point where they no longer have to
hire an outside conductor because they have developed their
own.

Laura's baton has many sides: patience; love; hard
knowledge, especially about system operation and management;
a profound grasp of human reality and an appreciation of human
uniqueness; and a keen sense of timeliness, coupled with an
ability to construct useful strategies.

Because this emanates from a clear sense of her own selfhood and a clear sense of others, there is a flow and naturalness in her writing and in her description of how she works. When the therapist is not clear about who he/she is, it is difficult to really see others, as it gets all mixed up. It sometimes results in the therapist treating him/herself, while calling it treating others. This is bound to end up in frustration and disappointment for both the therapist and the family.

Laura's method is to make the inharmonious, harmonious, thus creating balance and helping each member create his/her own unique music, while at the same time being in tune with the rest of the orchestra.

She clearly knows what nurturing and harmonious music sounds like, feels like, and looks like, as well as being familiar with its opposite.

To continue my analogy, Laura understands that when family members are not making harmonious music, it is likely to be because some instruments have stopped playing, and therefore have no voice; some blare out only discords, which irritate; some just play loud and drown out the rest; some play out of tune, which frustrates; some will play only solo, and some only duets. Laura obviously does not consider the problem one of bad instruments, but more of an education in understanding and using those instruments.

She shows the reader how she introduces each person to his/her own instrument without threat. She goes on to show how, as trust is built between herself and the family members, she creates a context in which each member is strongly invited to want to know how to play his/her own instrument. At the same time, he/she is being guided to an awareness of the depths of tone and the variety of expression that is his/her instrument's potential. She thus lays the groundwork for learning how to build and play with the other family members.

The outcome of this process is a full, fresh symphony written for the first time, played on tuned, loved, and understood instruments, and fitted to a specific purpose, design, and level of hearing that belongs to that particular orchestra.

In the usual orchestra, everyone literally knows the score. The orchestra leader merely brings it to life.

Not so for the orchestra leader of the family.

The family orchestra leader has to discover the yet unwritten symphony, write it with the family, and then free

vi

them to read their score and be able to develop new, harmonious arrangements when they are needed and wanted. Through this process, the members also learn to identify the sour notes and have choices about changing.

I consider the emphasis, which appears throughout the book, to be on the need for the family counselor to be in tune with, and in touch with, him/herself and with the others. Even the best orchestra leader is apt to fall flat on his face if he/she is not in touch with himself or his players, depending only on his technique.

Laura has shown in practice what I have urged all my students to do. She has taken in widely from the many rich resources that abound in our modern-day world relative to human growth and change. It is impressive that she has avoided the trap of being locked into any one theory or technique. She is not a GESTALTIST, a PSYCHODRAMATIST, a JUNGIAN, a SATIRIAN, or any other popular label today. Yet it is obvious that she has learned from and been influenced by these channels. Consequently, she can be free to use these learnings as resources when they fit, and build on her own experiences. The result is a rich, flexible, process-oriented, deeply humanistic, and realistic life-giving approach to helping troubled families, which I see as an approach that is ever becoming, not having become.

Laura's personal qualities of gentleness, strength, caring, and congruence, combined with her lucid style of writing and her practical content, make this book a powerful (in the sense of a seed) and important contribution to the practice of family therapy, for both the practitioner and the family.

Virginia Satir

February 1977

PREFACE

In these rapidly changing times, all systems and institutions are being seriously questioned as to their relevance to today's world. As an institution, the family, if it is to survive, must develop behaviors for patterning its existence which more closely approach today's needs.

In the writers' opinions, as long as quality development of the individual is an anticipated goal of life, the family must continue to exist. Whether or not the family maintains its traditional structure of husband/wife/children is a separate question. Defined as a unit of people sharing consistently in life's day-to-day functions and meeting daily needs of survival, love, and belonging, the family is fundamental in allowing individuals to move beyond basic survival needs toward the development of the potential of each family unit member.

The family is the primary environmental structure in which the child's learnings are integrated into day-by-day living. The quality of this core group interaction is a major influence on one's ability to transfer learnings and continue to develop potential in an ever-expanding environment.

The school is the institution most aligned with the task of the family--the development of the individual. Working hand-in-hand, the task of each institution is accomplished more fully and made easier by the investment of both the family and school.

Family counseling is exciting and creative work whereby influences are projected to the very foundations of the lives of individuals. While one cannot escape the confusion that results from change in basic institutions, one can, as a member of the counseling profession, share humanity's search for quality in core life groups which will contribute toward development of the individual, and which hopefully will do so with sufficient breadth, depth and humanness to make that contribution creative. In this sense, the field of family counseling is far more broad than that of providing a corrective process for malfunctioning in families and/or for facilitating the improvement of a child's functioning in a classroom.

By grasping the importance of the family in developing individuals who are self-actualizing (Maslow,1962,1971) and by envisioning the potential impact of this occurrence on today's

ix

world, the family counselor can begin to understand the broader aspects of the field.

The writers have undertaken to convey the creative possibilities of this field, so that hopefully the reader will experience his/her common humanity in the challenges of creative group living. Theory, technique, and process of family counseling are presented for the reader's use in developing his/her personal philosophy and style of working in family counseling.

This writing is presented in sections. A view of the potentials of family life is included in the first section. The second section outlines a conceptual framework for understanding families. The counselor's role with the family is discussed in the third section. The fourth section develops the process of family counseling and gives a complete case illustration demonstrating the actual processes and techniques used with a particular family. The fifth section offers a discussion of possible pitfalls or problem areas in family counseling.

The reader may choose to read the case first (beginning on page 55 and refer to the material of the earlier sections as the case references them, or he/she may choose to become acquainted with the conceptual base in the first three sections and then learn the practical application by reading the material in the sequence presented.

Thus the book is designed to be used both by practitioners and trainers. The conceptual and applied elements of the book were tested and integrated through the combined process of teaching, consulting and clinical practice. While the clinical setting was perhaps most influential in testing the system, many teaching professors, clinic directors, staff and graduate students also provided valuable insight and feedback. We are grateful for their sharing and support. The U.S. Office of Education, Pupil Personnel Services Division, should also be recognized for its awareness of the need to train trainers and trainers of trainers in the area of family counseling. In 1970-71 the authors were involved in a nationally focused training program which was funded to provide training for teaching professors and practitioners to develop family counseling concepts and competencies. Hopefully, these readers will recognize the similarily of the system from that time, as well as the modifications.

Laura Sue Dodson
DeWayne J. Kurpius

April 1977

TABLE OF CONTENTS

SECTION 3

SECTION 4

SECTION 5

LIST OF FIGURES

LIST OF TABLES

FAMILY COUNSELING: A SYSTEMS APPROACH

* *

Section **1**

A GROWTH MODEL

FOR

FAMILY LIFE

* *

A GROWTH MODEL FOR FAMILY LIFE

The family unit, broadly speaking, is a unit of people who live together and share life's basic day-by-day functions. Throughout history, humanity has demonstrated need for such a core group, yet also has demonstrated need for each individual member to grow. These dual, sometimes contrasting, human needs create the paradoxes of the family unit, in which exist struggle for separateness and togetherness, differentness and sameness, protection and freedom, support and independence.

THE FAMILY AND THE FAMILY LIFE PARADOX

The purpose of the family unit is to create a vessel or an environment for the development of mature, fully-functioning individuals. The paradox of the family situation is that this end is achieved only as the individuals in the family are contributing to and participating in the family process. When the family unit and an individual within this unit is confronted with an either/or situation, which would mean the satisfaction of one member at the expense of another member, growth barriers tend to be created. In effect, this either/or situation is resolved at the expense of both, since the well-being of the two is indivisible. At the highest level of complementary coexistence, conflict and resolution occur without an either/or mandate: rather the conflict and resolution occur within a process of mutual nurturing of growth. The conceptual framework on which this writing is based and with which this section is particularly concerned is that in order for a family to function at the complementary coexistence level, it must operate within a "growth framework."

3

"The Paradox of the Family Unit"

THE GROWTH FRAMEWORK

When operating in a growth framework, family members accept as an ever-existing fact that tension, at times, will exist between needs of individuals and needs of the core group. Family members confront these issues as the issues appear in the life process and the members deal with each incident without any necessity of precedents or patterns for behavior.

When a family is not in a growth framework, seemingly arbitrary decisions might be made, and such decisions may have little to do with the present, or may be made on the basis of low self-esteem in the individuals involved. Family members may seem to be immune to the influence of new data, and rigid stances of behavior may be observed. When decisions must be made, individuals may approach the situation without a process of shared ideas or feelings or input of information, and instead proceed with absolute certainty of the correct outcome. The attitude may be "don't bother me with the facts." The process which then follows reflects an effort to make behavior match expected outcomes.

In a growth framework, externally or internally super-imposed behaviors do not determine interaction or decision, instead the family is involved in a _process_ of interaction in which current data and feelings are considered in decision making. Allowances exist for each person's ideas, anticipating difference and/or compromise. Flexibility must occur both in behavior and attitude which allows for evolution of decisions appropriate to particular people and circumstances at a particular time. Outcomes frequently are not as important as the processes involved in the reaching of these outcomes. A family operating in a growth framework cannot be recognized readily by _what_ the outcomes are, but is sooner revealed by _how_ these outcomes are accomplished.

In a growth framework when events or stimuli occur involving family members, the members do not react by retreating from one another, by fearing self-disclosure, or by avoiding confrontation and discussion. Instead, family members attempt to become aware of their own feelings and thoughts and they feel free to share or not share these feelings, as appropriate to the situation at the time. Members can choose to reveal themselves openly to one another without fear of rejection or blame. However, they also may choose not to be open with each other in a growth framework, but not for such a secondary purpose as avoiding feared expectations. Members can be apart or together, as is fitting for each individual. Members sense their potential availability, commitment and uncon-

5

ditional love to others, a feeling which aids them in their
growth process.

In a growth framework, each individual assumes responsibility for one's own behavior. Even with the youngest child,
a growing sense of personal responsibility for behavior is
evident. Statements such as "I did it when Dad told me
to . . ." are more likely to be made than "Dad made me do it."

To the degree that a family is operating in a growth
framework, it is described by this author as an "actualizing
family." Of course, families are not either actualizing or
non-actualizing, operating in a growth framework or not
operating in a growth framework; rather, one can say family
actualization occurs in a process of family growth and development. Families become more actualizing in direct relation to
the self-actualization of members.

FAMILY GROWTH PROCESS AND FAMILY ACTUALIZATION

Operating in an actualizing manner is a more frequent
occurrence as the family is attending to its hierarchy of
needs. The family has basic needs that must be met in the
process of family growth. These needs can be paralleled to the
individual need hierarchy described by Maslow, (1962) in his
book, Toward a Psychology of Being. The family need hierarchy
may be expressed as follows:

Survival. The family has a need to survive together. On
a biological level, a need exists for food, shelter, and
clothing. Emotionally, the family needs to survive and
feel secure as an intact system, while at the same time
its individuals survive and feel secure in continuing
their individuation process.

Belonging Needs. The family has a need to feel a basic
sense of belonging together, a feeling that, within the
family unit, everyone has a place. The family unit also
needs to feel that it belongs in the larger system of the
community. Individuals in the family need a sense of
being loved by other members and need to feel love toward
other members.

Esteem. The family needs esteem for itself. Family
members must have respect for their existence together
and for their common purposes and goals. The family needs
to value its struggles and pleasures. To gain this
esteem, each family member attempts to understand the
interaction of the family and hopes that the interaction
holds meaning that once understood, can be respected in
the context of that person's life and the family life.

6

Need to Actualize. Family members have a need to enhance their personal growth and the growth of others in the family unit, and to pool knowledge, skill, feeling, intuition, and uniqueness to evolve a system of inter-action which will facilitate and enrich the individuation process in a way which the individual cannot accomplish alone.

Once needs are being satisfied at lower or primary levels in a fairly consistent manner, families, like individuals, naturally yearn for and need development on the higher levels of increased family esteem and increased family actualization.

PEAK EXPERIENCES IN AN ACTUALIZING FAMILY

Peak family experiences occur when family members maintain their separate identities and simultaneously can go beyond selfhood and feel as one with others. The differentiation of self from others has been basically resolved so striving toward it is no longer important. Movement toward individuation* and being one's full and unrestrained self in the presence of others who are doing the same must occur. And this movement occurs within a climate of mutual appreciation and respect. These contributing factors allow the possibility of a peak experience of self/other acutalization to occur. For example, the mother can feel as one with her child, and a couple can come closer to what Buber (1970) calls an "I-Thou" relation-ship. Both parents and children can richly experience new awareness of themselves and each other in the moment. This experience is the height of family actualization. As families become more actualizing (operate more in a growth framework), such experiences occur more frequently within the units. (See example in case, p. 113.)

A family may be tempted to strive for a state of actu-alizing and reaching peak experiences, neglecting the foundations and evolutions necessary for these to occur. Or they may try to "hang on" to such experiences or to reproduce them. Ironically, perhaps, such experiences cannot be sought or created. These experiences can only evolve, usually with a certain element of surprise, as individuals tend to their own

---

*"Individuation" is a Jungian term referring to the develop-ment of the individual (Jung, 1933). Jung's use of the word "individuation" is similar to Maslow's (1962, 1971) use of the term "self-actualization." These two terms are used inter-changeably in this text.

growth processes and as families become more actualizing in day-by-day, moment-by-moment behaviors. For an example of a family peak experience see pp. 111-113.

GUIDELINES TOWARD FAMILY ACTUALIZATION

Actualizing family systems cannot happen simply because the members love one another or have good intentions toward one another; nor does actualizing fail to happen because people are bad or wrong. Instead, the degree of actualizing within a family is determined by where the members are in their own growth and development and where, in growth, the family system is.

Family actualization is enhanced by the development of self-esteem in individuals within the family. This actualization evolves as one feels a positive view toward one's own and toward others' potentials and as members feel respect for one another. Further, only those families can experience actualization whose members are willing to deal with the duality of needs of self and systems and therefore are willing to invest some of their life energy into the quality of development of both.

For a family to be actualizing, members must not allow the system itself to gain power, life, and momentum of its own beyond its function as a vessel to contain individuals as they grow and change. The nature of the family system must not demand that individuals be in continual service to the maintenancy of the system at the limitation of personal growth. Rather, the major emphasis in the actualizing family is that the system is in service to the individuals within the family unit. This means that the system must change as individual needs change. A reversal to dysfunctional behavior may occur when individuals misuse the family.

NON-ACTUALIZING FAMILIES AND DYSFUNCTIONAL BEHAVIOR

A family, by virtue of its existence as a group of persons living together with depth of intrapsychic involvement, is vulnerable to misuse by its members. For example, the family can be misused as a place for any of the following:

1. For an individual to subscribe to family role expectations rather than enter into the struggle for one's own identity through self-development.

2. For a member to project one's problems on others.

8

3. For an individual to invest energy in maintaining a rigid position in the family such as (a) the boss, (b) the bossed one or the placator, (c) the rescuer of others in the family, (d) the keeper of the family or societal rules, and (e) the distractor, or the irrelevant one.

With these occurrences (many more could be cited), an environment is created that is conducive to limitation of individual growth. The resulting family system will be characterized by rigid behaviors and tend to limit, if not stifle, individual growth. Under such conditions the family, then, operates in direct opposition to an individual's natural inclination toward development of one's potential.

The process of family actualization and self-actualization is not easy. In fact, frequently the process is stressful and creates an environment of living with insecurity. When each incident is met without behavioral precedent, one cannot know what will happen next. One individual does not control others. Each is open to the movement and growth life offers; therefore, one must be alert and adaptive and make fresh decisions as circumstances change.

The nature of pain and distress in the process of actualization is a completely different experience than that of pain and distress as a consequence of a rigid family system. The former carries with it a tinge of excitement and hope. The experiences may be said to "hurt good." In the rigid system, an absence of hope and an overlay of feeling trapped and defeated is evident.

To the degree that families are not actualizing, family members develop maladaptive or ineffective interaction. This condition is revealed by ineffective communication. Further, periodic physical illnesses of various members may occur as Lewis (1976) notes in his study of well families. The dysfunctional family may produce a "symptom bearer," that is a member who signals pain in the family by malfunctioning in the community, the school and/or at home.

Then family distress does occur which is related to a halt in the growth of its members and the lack of a growth framework in its system, as best as it can, the family unit uses whatever tools it has to deal with the problems. Family members do not wish to cause pain to themselves or one another. Behavior of family members toward each other, regardless of how ineffective or even cruel it may seem, is, in the deepest sense of its motivation, an attempt to "make things right."

Sometimes an attempted solution to a problem is helpful in rechanneling the family toward a growth framework and actualization. At other times, the effort adds further complications and more symptoms develop or those present become more intense. When these conditions occur, input from outside the family in the form of education or counseling may be necessary to assist the family in removing obstacles preventing individual and family growth.

* *

Section **2**

CONCEPTUAL FRAMEWORKS

FOR

UNDERSTANDING FAMILIES

* *

CONCEPTUAL FRAMEWORKS FOR UNDERSTANDING FAMILIES

Family counseling is a meeting ground of two conceptual frameworks: (1) that in which individuals are a product of their environment, and (2) that wherein individuals create their environment. In family counseling both factors are embraced. Thus, the family counselor must have an understanding of the two conceptual frameworks--family systems as well as individual dynamics.

Further, inasmuch as communication is the main connector in human interaction systems, communication is a major tool in counseling with families. Therefore, imperatively the family counselor must understand the dynamics of human communication.

The family undergoes what is termed crises. Crises are a normal part of family life. When they occur, they tend to force the system into change or to resistance of change. The counselor, working with families, needs knowledge of family life crises and modes of dealing with crises.

The counselor then, for maximum effectiveness, needs knowledge of four conceptual frameworks in order to make an assessment of family problems and to counsel with families. These four conceptual frameworks are the following:

1. Family systems

2. Individual dynamics

3. Communication

4. Crises

The first, family systems, and last, crises, are discussed in the writing that follows. For the purpose of this brief writing, the assumption is made that the reader has

13

previous knowledge of the fields of human communication and
individual dynamics. The reader may refer to the Bibliography
at the conclusion of this writing for a further study of these
areas. The case example, however, in Section IV illustrates
the practical use of all four conceptual frameworks.

FAMILY SYSTEMS CHARACTERISTICS

Family systems are composed of <u>individuals</u> who interact
within usually nonverbally agreed upon <u>rules or patterns</u> of
behavior and with a <u>range of flexibility</u> to their behaviors.
The system offers certain <u>limitations and rewards</u> to its
members and requires some degree of equilibrium for its functioning. A family system operates within a present, past and
future <u>context</u>. These six factors are the characteristics of
a family system (Satir, 1972).

Understanding the characteristics of a family system
offers a structured means of assessing interaction within a
family as well as providing a vehicle for understanding the
meaning of behavior. Further, such an understanding provides
a means by which to define aspects of a family that are tending
toward a growth framework and those that tend to inhibit
growth.*

No ideal characteristics for all family systems exist.
Each system is as unique as each individual within that system.
The hope for every family is that members will find the system
of interaction that best facilitates the growth of individuals
in that particular family. Growth-enhancing family systems are
not static. Characteristics of these families must change as
individuals in the family change and as influencing factors in
the environment change. The six characteristics of a family
system are discussed in this section.

_____

*As the counselor seeks understanding of behavior in family
systems, a need exists to recognize that one cannot always
become aware of the meaning of behavior. One must recognize
that individuals and groups are immensely complex and probably
one will never be able to understand every aspect of the
behaviors. This complexity is part of both the frustration and
the excitement of the field. The framework is offered as a
guideline to assessing and counseling with families and is not
to be used to push the unending nuances and complexities of
human beings into a reductive and rigid framework.

Individuals

Individuals within the family system have their own internal system, composed of the same characteristics as the family system. A family system can only become actualizing in direct relation to the degree that the individuals have developed an internal system that allows for their actualization. Satir (1972) stressed that the self-actualization of the parents is the foundation on which the quality of the family system is built. The reader is referred particularly to Satir (1972), Maslow (1962, 1971) Rogers (1967) and Jung (1928-1964) as listed in the Bibliography for discussion of the individual.

Rules Or Patterns Of Behavior

Rules provide the skeleton or core indicator of the nature of a family's system. Rules are nonverbally agreed upon behaviors that usually are implied rather than explicitly stated and are frequently outside the awareness of family members. Once a family becomes aware of the family's own rules, however, choices become feasible. Family members may then participate more consciously in forming rules that are more facilitating to the growth of each individual. Dysfunctional rules are rules which operate within a rigid framework, misusing the family. Growth-enhancing rules reflect a growth framework and allow for self and family actualization.

Some areas in which rules exist in all families and examples of dysfunctional and growth-enhancing rules are presented in Table 1.

TABLE 1. EXAMPLES OF FAMILY RULES

Area of Rule	Dysfunctional Example	Growth Enhancing Example
Who can talk to whom? About what may one speak?	If the child wants Father to know something about the child, then the child tells Mother and she tells Father.	One may talk to the person about whom a reaction is experienced or with whom one wishes to discuss thoughts or feelings. One also may choose not to do so, but the reason is not to protect or enhance self-esteem.
When and how may a member go away from this family to relate to others? Or to be alone?	If one is alone or prefers to be with others, that individual is suspected of not caring about family members or of being angry.	Going in and out of this family has to do with individual and family needs as these needs occur. The behavior is not used to send indirect messages nor is it interpreted in a stereotyped way.
When and how may a member manifest difference from another and similarity to another? How can one be unique? And how, when, and where may one show that uniqueness?	1. Obscure any difference between family members. 2. Maintain individual areas of autonomy at all costs. 3. Appear to disagree or to agree even when one does not.	One is free to allow self to develop uniqueness as a human being; whether that be similar to or different from another is not relevant. Pleasures can be shared while one remains a unique self and, in fact, pleasures can be enhanced by integrity.

Table 1. Continued, page 2

Area of Rule	Dysfunctional Example	Growth Enhancing Example
What, when and how may one comment on what one sees, feels and thinks?	1. Do not ask questions, particularly in areas of sensitivity.	One may comment about anything one sees, feels, or thinks, upon choice. (One values self and others, and considers the context in making choices.) Judging one another's perceptions is not an issue, and ulterior motives are not present in statements.
	2. Do not say what one really thinks and feels; or imply that that feeling is acceptable.	
	3. One must always comment about all things seen, felt and thought. All must be family property.	Responses of others to what one says are heard as additional information and are perceptions not lessening the value of self or the persons who offer such responses.
How may one show feelings such as love, hurt, and anger? How may one receive those feelings from another?	1. Do not express pain verbally.	One may express or refrain from expressing, but one does not make the choice based on ulterior motives or reasons related to self-esteem.
	2. Do not express anger.	
	3. Be careful how much caring is expressed; one might embarrass someone.	One may listen to and hear feelings as expressed by others and when one hears conflicting messages, one is free to comment on these. One may feel opposite reactions to the same person.
	4. One must continually express love feelings, whether they are felt or not, to make certain of avoiding offending in any way.	

Table 1. Continued, page 3

Area of Rule	Dysfunctional Example	Growth Enhancing Example
How and when may one let needs and wants be known to another? When and how may one respond to the needs and wants of others?	1. Everyone should be self-sufficient. If needs take the upper hand, apologize for having them before asking for help. 2. If one responds to another's needs, then one wears the label "strong" and the other will wear the label "weak" or vice-versa. 3. Do not say what is wanted for self. 4. Always express every need or want and demand its fulfillment, regardless of the circumstances.	Everyone in the family may be allowed to be aware of needs and wants without judgment. These needs can be expressed without fear of rejection for having needs and wants. What needs and wants are met is communsurate with the present context and the choices of others. These decisions are not viewed as a comment on self or other's worth but, rather, as simply the present situation.
How may one feel and express sexuality?	1. Sexuality is not to be mentioned. Act as if it does not exist. 2. Adults may be sexual; children, regardless of age, may not. 3. Sexuality is always the major facet of one's being and must always be expressed.	Sexuality is an important part of life and sexual feelings are acceptable. As such, these feelings need not be hidden or expressed by a rigid rule, but by choice, as is appropriate to the context and not as related to fear of unacceptability.

18

Table 1. Continued, page 4

Area of Rule	Dysfunctional Examples	Growth Enhancing Examples
How may one gain self-esteem and how much may one have?	1. Self-esteem is related to how well one follows the family rules. 2. Children may not surpass their parents in self-esteem.	Self-esteem is not diminished by attack or blame; it is a basic ingredient of an actualizing family, and when one's esteem is low, the individual, as well as others around, may attempt to support positively his/her innate worth as a person.
How may one grow and change in another's presence?	1. One must be in continual change. One may not do the same thing twice. 2. Change should be controlled so that people remain as similar as possible to how they have been in the past.	Movement toward further realization of one's potential is to be celebrated; and retreat, when retreat is fitting for foundation building and integration, is also honored by the family. Attempts to grow and change include respect for one another's and one's own processes in life.
How may one be a man or a woman and a human being?	1. Men always . . . . . 2. All women	One follows his/her own inner guide toward self-actualization, and family members support one another in the individual's efforts to do so.

19

Range Of Flexibility

Every family has a degree of variation from family rules or patterns of behavior that allows the system to continue to function without the development of a crisis. For example, a rule may prevent unwanted conflict from emerging. The rule may serve to render a subject mute but without resolution. (Rule example: We will attempt to ignore and certainly not talk about our feelings about mom and dad separating.) Perhaps the family fears that if the rule is broken, conflict will come into the open again; some event or feeling which members consider intolerable will be experienced, such as an argument, or separation, or renewal of old hurts. The behavior pattern is needed, then, and perhaps desperately needed as the family perceives the situation, in order for the family to continue to function. Obviously, in such a case, the rule to prevent unwanted conflict would have little flexibility.

Some flexibility is required in the face of normal crises of life if the family is to maintain some degree of well being. The more actualizing the system, the more the rules are sufficiently flexible to adapt to changing situations, circumstances and needs.

Limitations And Rewards

Adherence to the system rules or behavior patterns results in rewards to the individual and the family. The rewards as perceived by members must be greater than the limitations on family life.

An example of a reward might be security. The cost may be rigid limitations on self-expression, thus, also on personal growth and learning. The same rigid limitations, however, also may be seen as rewards of the system by persons who want the security of being protected against their uniqueness. However, such a reward would render the family dysfunctional to some degree.

Equilibrium

Every family sustains some sense of equilibrium and tolerates a degree of disequilibrium before symptoms of dysfunction begin to develop. A family is constantly thrown off balance as it interacts within itself and with the world, as changes occur in areas such as age, life experience, health and work. Every change affects the equilibrium of the family system. A family system operating in a growth framework will have a greater range of possible behaviors before members experience disequilibrium. Members will have flexibility in

20

their rules. Normal life crises, for example, can be experienced while maintaining equilibrium.

Context

Context refers to the time, place, and situation of a particular family interaction, and to the history of the system. Context also refers to the family's future hopes and goals.

Present Time, Place, and Situation. Time refers to the actual period during which a process occurs. For example, the time between the arrival home of the family members and when dinnertime occurs is considered by Jackson (1968) in Communication, Family and Marriage, Human Communication, Vol. I, to be the period most potentially destructive to a family. Family members may be tired; simultaneously they are in the process of making a transition from the systems of which they have been a part during the day, to the family system. Behavior must be understood in light of these factors.

interface transition

Time also refers to stages of life. Family members are faced with different developmental tasks at different stages in their lives. (See pp. 23-25.) The time of various stages of development must be considered in understanding the meaning of behavior. Different rules and patterns of behavior are needed at different stages of family life.

Place affects behavior. For example, a family may have one set of rules and patterns for behavior at home and another set for school, or another standard of behavior for grandmother's house.

The situational context of behavior refers to the combination of circumstances at a specific time. For example, when a mother is relaxed and emotionally available to the child she may respond one way; when she is depressed, or when three other children want her attention as well, she may respond quite differently to the same behavior from the same child. Situational context also may refer to broader situational factors outside the family which influence family behavior, such as wars or national economic conditions.

HISTORY OF THE SYSTEM

Each family system has its own unique history. The unique nature of any family is influenced by the parents, who are the architects of the family. The parents come to their union at a certain point in their personal growth. The parents bring with them models from their pasts that influence their

"Within the family, normal crisis
occur as the family members
change in age, which in turn
changes needs of individuals in
the family unit . . ."

behaviors. The unique system of a particular family is formed in part as a result of members acting from influences of these experiences from their pasts. The current power and influence of these notions may not be within the awareness of the family. Helping to bring history and its current power into a family's awareness created an opportunity for re-learning or unlearning in a family. This understanding gives the family members an opportunity of basing present interactions on present contexts when controls of the past have been growth-inhibiting. This growth opportunity provides for including past awarenesses when the historical influences are growth-enhancing.

FUTURE HOPES AND GOALS

A family's present interaction may be governed by future hopes. For example, mother will not cuddle her seven year old when the child has been hurt and seems to want to be cuddled because she wants him/her to be self-sufficient and she believes cuddling the child will make him/her a dependent adult. In this example, the mother's hope for the future determines her present actions. When future hopes and goals control behavior to the degree that present context is ignored, maladaptive behavior may result. In Section 4, pp. 95-99, the assessment of a family is shown by these system characteristics.

CRISIS IN FAMILY LIFE*

Crises are a normal part of family life. Crises may occur when situations outside the family change, such as forced or sudden change in location of living, or in job, natural disasters such as floods, or when socio-political problems such as economic depression occur. Within the family, normal crises occur as the family members change in age, which in turn changes needs of individuals in the family unit as they grow and change psychologically, and as members' health and physical needs may change. All crises affecting the family demand alterations in the family system. Crises occurring in normal family life development are discussed by Erikson (1959, p. 35) and summarized as follows:

Marriage. The couple now have the task of relinquishing original family systems and establishing patterns of the

---

*A crisis in the family life refers to events or happenings outside or inside the family unit, which upset the traditional ways of interacting, thus demanding change in the family system.

marriage relationship. The degree to which separation from the previous system successfuly occurs is a major factor in the quality of the new system.

Child Bearing. The couple must sustain the development of their own marriage and continue its growth while simultaneously beginning the construction of parent-child relationships. Branching out into parenting when the marriage relationship has not been stabilized is a common problem at this crisis time. Further, at the stage of child bearing, a second or third birth can and often does occur before the integration of the first child into the system has sufficient adjustment to allow the system to regain a healthy equilibrium.

Last Child Enters School. Parents, particularly the mother, must realign personal roles and a child must expand into a new world at the time school is entered.

Adolescence of the First Child. As the first child reaches adolescence, the family must provide opportunity for protection and nurture for this child's growth pattern. At the same time, the family must provide for separateness and individuation.

Last Child Leaves Home. When the last child leaves home, this stage of family life development requires that the parent-child relationship be changed by establishing adult-to-adult relationships between parents and their children. The parents' marriage relationship enters another stage. Deepening and expanding the relationship is a challenge at this time, as well as is further personal development of both husband and wife.

Aging. Integration and reflection are a part of the aging process necessary to complete the full circle of life itself. Family participation in this process can allow for growth of all members. This approach is in opposition to our societal practice of ignoring the facts that life presupposes death, that we do age, and that we do go through important processes during the aging years which are worthy of being in our awareness and fully experienced. Unfortunately family members' fears and denials of death often cause the family to ignore these most essential and potentially creative processes of aging.

Just as a family gains a comfortable equilibrium and establishes well-functioning rules in one stage of development, another stage is entered, creating a new crisis in the system, and demanding change once more. Life is never static.

Crisis resolution in one development stage becomes the foundation on which the next crisis is met. While normal life crises may be used as opportunities for family and individual growth, if ineffectively handled these crises could produce a secondary crisis, causing dysfunctional patterns of behavior to result.

PATTERNS FOR DEALING WITH FAMILY CRISIS

In a maladaptive pattern of dealing with crisis, a more rigid, less growth-enhancing system develops as a result of the crisis. In such a pattern, no process of family inter-action for crisis resolution is experienced. Crises are handled by means of superimposed structures. Should these structures be ineffective, a secondary crisis develops out of the family dysfunctioning.

This maladaptive pattern can be seen in the case of the child who created a crisis by running away from home. If the parents are contemplating divorce, for example, they are forced into a unity again to deal with the crisis created by the child. In this instance, the running away is not the core problem, but rather the result of how the family is dealing with the crisis of marital discord.

A maladaptive pattern of dealing with crisis results in a new equilibrium within the system after crisis, often at the price of further growth limitations on the family as well as on individual members. (See p. 95.) However, the pattern, though maladaptive, does represent the family's best effort at problem resolution using the tools accessible to them at that time.

A second pattern for dealing with crises is a coping or adaptive approach. In this manner, change is carefully regulated so that when crises occur a minimal upset and a rapid return to the status quo is facilitated. Past experi-ences or future goals are used to solve present crises. This pattern is growth-enhancing when a family actually needs a period of status quo for integration. It is growth-inhibiting, however, when equilibrium and status quo become the highest consistent priority.

At times persons in such a system can be benefited by allowing an upset in equilibrium to occur, thereby creating an opportunity to offset some problem areas with new behaviors and new growth. Coping with or adapting to crises in order to keep the status quo has both strengths and limitations. Un-less referred by an outside source, a counselor may never

25

reach the family that consistently applies the coping/adaptive
approach to crises, since usually the family members do not
experience sufficient discomfort to motivate the family to
secure counseling.

Creative approaches to crises can occur when crises are
used as opportunities for growth. Using crises as opportunities for growth is difficult for most people for many
reasons. At the moment of pain brought by crisis, fear is
many times present. The past system though it may not have
been the most productive, had its virtues, not the least of
which was familiarity and predictability. That system offered
a measure of security. Further, the nature of systems makes
the process of seeing change as an opportunity for growth a
difficult response. Systems tend to gain a life and momentum
of their own, which sometimes seem stronger than individual
family members. Maslow (1971) in his book, The Farther Reaches
of Human Nature, describes a man emerging, who is able to use
crises for expansion:

> We must develop a new kind of human being . . .
> (who will) not (be) afraid of change but rather
> be able to . . . enjoy change . . . They must be
> people who will not fight change but anticipate
> it . . . and be challenged by it. We need people
> different from the average kind of person who
> confronts the present as if it were a repetition of
> the past, and who uses the present simply as a
> period in which to prepare for future . . . We
> need an increased ability to pay fullest attention
> to the here and now situation, to be able to listen
> well . . . and to see the immediate moment before
> us . . . to trust ourselves to handle the problem
> in an improvising way . . . divorcing (our) selves
> from the past.

To use family crisis for growth is an experience in family
actualization. The more a family is operating in a growth
framework, the more crises can be used for growth.

An example of a family using a crisis for growth follows:

> A woman loses her husband through sudden death. Her
> children are adults. The mourning experience may
> increase the family's ability to share deep feelings.
> This can become a new pattern of behavior in their
> relationships, continuing after the crisis. Further,
> the absence of the husband-father can create new
> areas for relating between the mother and her adult
> children. It creates a time of self-examination of
> values and life goals that may offer change of a

positive nature to individuals and to the system. If a family is able to experience the positive changes the crisis has caused and can allow the system to incorporate constructive change, the family has used the crisis in an actualizing way. (Maslow, 1971)

To employ creative approaches to family crises when integration is needed would be a maladaptive pattern. Coping or adaptive patterns are then more appropriate. The actualizing family maintains a creative tension between integration and growth and does not seek growth and creativity at the price of integration loss.

The counselor will need to know the normal life crises occurring in the family at the time the family comes for counseling, as well as secondary crises that may have occurred because of low-level resolutions to normal life crises. (See example pp. 92-93.) A counselor will need to know how the family functioned before the more recent crisis and whether or not this type of functioning is the norm the family members aspire to regain. Knowing the family's usual methods for dealing with crises and knowing the nature of the present crisis will also help the counselor know how the family is functioning in relation to family hierarchy of needs. This information will help the counselor approach the family at the level of their present growth and development. Further, the counselor needs to be aware that poorly resolved crises in the parents' childhood may contribute subsequently to a child's difficulty in resolving similar crises in the child's growth and development. (See pp. 92-93.)

* *

Section **3**

THE FAMILY COUNSELOR

* *

THE FAMILY COUNSELOR

Above all else, the counselor is the most important factor in family counseling. Personal development, personal awareness and the use of self are basic to the counselor's effectiveness with a family. In Section III these areas are discussed, as well as the various roles the counselor assumes in his/her work.

THE COUNSELOR AND HIS/HER SELF-DEVELOPMENT

The counselor's effectiveness is demonstrated as much, if not more, by how he/she interacts with the family than by what is said. While the counselor needs knowledge of family systems, individual dynamics, communication and crises, of no less importance is the fine tuning of the best instrument-- himself/herself. The counselor needs to be in a constant process of becoming an aware human being in the fullest sense of the word "aware."*

In order to be aware of what is occurring during inter- action in a family, the counselor needs to see far more than spoken words in the interaction or intellectual concepts about

---

*AWARE by Webster's definition implies vigilance in observing as well as in drawing accurate inferences from what one sees, hears and feels. Aware refers to having knowledge of something that is not obvious or apparent. Synonyms of "aware" are cognizant, conscious, sensible, alive and awake. Cognizant implies special knowledge; consciousness implies awareness at the level of full attention; sensibility implies the full use of all senses operating together; alive adds to the definition of sensible an acute sensitivity; and awake denotes alertness.

familes. The need exists to allow images, spontaneous
thoughts and feelings to come into awareness, and to trust the
intuitive impressions to enhance one's own understanding. By
so doing, the counselor is able to experience, on a trans-
personal level, an intuitive knowledge beyond what is being
discussed. These levels of understanding are gained through
the counselor's self-development.

Image Thinking means seeing that which is being discussed.
Image thinking means that the counselor develops imagination
and ability to think visually. As the counselor listens to
family members talk, visualizations occur as to what they are
saying. As an example, the counselor may visualize action
words. If the statement is made, "My Dad is just running off
at the mouth," the counselor's visual image might be of the
father actually running away by means of words. Looking at
the expression as a visual image introduces the possibility of
seeing how words create distance, in this case between the
father and the son. By using the visual image as an indicator
of directions in counseling, frequently issues basic to the
family conflict quickly emerge. (See further examples in the
case presented on pp. 83-85, 105-107.) By developing the
ability to think visually and pay attention to the counselor's
own visual images, regardless of how unrelated they may at
first appear, the counselor is aided in transcending the
limitations of words and moving to the essence of an individual's experience or a family's interaction.

Spontaneous thoughts and feelings of the counselor, when
made a part of the counseling process, may further aid the
counselor in moving to the essence of the family conflict.
The counselor may be angry, or amused, feel sad, or excited or
bored, or may have any number of physical responses to the
counseling situation, such as nausea or headache. For example,
a counselor may feel angry at the behavior of one family member
toward another. By recognizing this response and revealing it
in a timing that can be received, the counselor may find that
other family members as well have long been angry at this
behavior. The family member has not confronted the person, but
rather has allowed negative control to happen in the family.
(For further examples see case study on pp. 77, 131.)

Self-awareness is essential to the family counselor. The
counselor needs to be conscious of personal areas of conflict.
All of the counselor's personal problems need not be solved,
of course, as this is never totally possible for any human.
(Individuals are in constant evolvement but never fully aware.
This evolvement is part of the limitation as well as the
challenge of being human!) The counselor will need to have a
"feel" for personal strengths and limitations and an awareness
of the present stage of his or her personal growth. This

awareness can allow one to be awake to the overlap of personal psychology with that of the counselees. As a counselor learns when his/her intuitions and feelings relate to the current situation in counseling in a significant way and when these feelings are more related to self than to the counseling situation, then the counselor becomes better equipped to determine when and how one's intuitive impressions and feelings are useful in counseling and can avoid, for the most part, projecting personal conflicts on others. When a counselor can be aware of self as well as aware of others, the counselor's own human responses have been added as working tools.

Being cognizant of one's own limitations can aid the counselor in accepting personal errors in judgment and awkwardness or misdirection in counseling, all of which inevitably happen. Such awareness and self-acceptance lessen the pressure for perfection that can be an occupational hazard of this profession. These traits afford the opportunity of sharing one's common humanness with the counselees. Self-awareness can further increase the counselor's comfort with self. He/she is less apt to be alarmed by or condemning of personal emotional responses to the counseling situation; thus, the counselor allows personal intuitive and feeling responses to be more fully in awareness. Access then is available to more of self in the counseling situation.

The Counselor's Awareness Of Own Family System

Awareness of one's own family system is necessary for the family counselor. The counselor needs to know what roles are played in the counselor's family and the similarities between these roles and personal behavior today; how these are communicated and the relevance of that information today; and how the system of one's own family might be described. Working with families that have similar systems to that of the counselor's family likely will evoke the most emotional reaction in the counselor. Working with families similar to one's own will stretch the edge of the counselor's own growth.

Aids In Self And System Awareness

Self and family system awareness can be enhanced by application of the information related in this section to one's self. The counselor may apply the techniques described in the case material of Section IV to self and own family system by drawing personal internal parts in various situations. (See p. 119.) For example, the counselor may describe the characteristics of the family system at various significant times in personal life. (See pp. 14-21.) The counselor may role play various conflicting situations (See pp. 47-48.) to further understanding of self and own family system. Further, the counselor may ask for feedback from family and friends to assist in seeing how others perceive him/her.

Counseling For The Counselor

This writer feels that counseling for the counselor is of basic importance to the development of the art of counseling. Experiencing the counseling process can help reach dimensions of self and system awareness and personal development, unattainable by self-help methods. Further, as the counselee, the process of counseling itself is experienced emotionally to add to one's intellectual learning. To experience being on the other side of the fence gives one a kind of empathy with the counselee's struggles unattainable in any other way. The counselor's personal growth, though, is the main objective of the counseling experience. Because the counselor's main tool in counseling is self, attending to personal development and enrichment is basic not only to personal life, but also to the professional work itself.

Supervision For The Counselor

The opportunity to discuss one's work with others can further afford personal and professional growth. The counselor's emotional responses to families, when examined, help to further self-understanding and, thus, further tunes the fine instrument of counseling--self.

Conclusion On The Counselor And Self-Development

While a counselor needs to be aware of both self and the family in a counseling situation, no dichotomy is implied between the attention a counselor is directing toward the family in a session and that which is being directed toward self. Attention to both self and the counseled family simultaneously should become habit and be standard background to whatever content is being discussed.

When a counselor can be aware of self in the presence of others, he/she has combined personal human response with other working tools. Then the counselor has available not merely personal intellectual processes of theory and technique, but emotional reactions to what is happening as well.

Without exception, when a counselor has a high degree of self and other awareness, has developed ability to think in images, and can spontaneously be aware of personal thoughts and feelings and follow these as guides in counseling (letting techniques fall in line with internal responses), the counselor will experience a high degree of effectiveness in

34

counseling. At the highest level of functioning in this
manner, the counselor will have a self-actualizing experience.

THE COUNSELOR'S ROLES

The counselor assumes many roles in the counseling
process. Defining these roles is a necessary part of
providing an understanding foundation for this writing.

The Band-Aid Or Truant Officer

In cases of critical and urgent family situations, a
counselor may be forced toward immediate action in order to
save life, protect well-being, prevent the commission of crime,
or comply with the law. The need for this type of judgment
may be quite suddenly imposed on a counselor, and the counselor
may have no viable choice but to forego the counseling process
and make decisions for the person or persons involved. Although accepting this decisive role is a legitimate function
of the counselor, this role demands, for the most part, relinquishing the counseling process described in this writing. A
counselor should consider this role as an extreme facet of the
responsibility in working with a family.

Other Eyes, Other Ears, Other Senses

A major role for the counselor in every phase of counseling is to provide an additional perception of the family, one
which can help the family see more clearly what is happening
in their personal system. Acting in conjunction with a family,
a counselor assesses and describes (does not judge) the nature
of the interaction in the family's particular group. As this
function is performed, the counselor, in effect, is affording
the family "new lenses," since the family often may be viewing
their situation with "tunnel vision." That is, the family
views the system, its problems, and its solutions from a
limited perspective, which may complicate the problem. Further,
in helping a family to bring into focus their view of the
problem more clearly and to gain a perspective that facilitates
solutions, a counselor simultaneously allows the family to
catch sight of resources they personally possess for dealing
with their own situation. (See example p. 113.)

Teacher

Helping families to see and to better understand what is
happening in their system is a process of educating families.
Like a teacher, a counselor must be able to coordinate the
giving of information with the timing of that sharing for
learning to take place. The counselor works only with the

parts of the assessment which are confirmed by the family:
that is, only with the joint assessments made. As the family
learns to see their own system, emotionally and intellectually,
they are able to become aware of patterns of behavior that
cause them pain and to gain the tools necessary to change
these patterns. (See pp. 103, 113.)

Environmental "Acclimator"

The counselor has the task of creating and maintaining a
safe environment for change, one in which people can risk to
be different, try new behaviors, and express those thoughts
and feelings they once considered inexpressible. This task
calls for the application of growth-enhancing rules during the
sessions. A counselor strives toward creating a model of an
actualizing system--the system which the counselor and the
family as a unit compose (See pp. 61-67.) As well, the counselor strives to model growth-enhancing behaviors by his/her
own attitudes and communications. The counselor may further
model a growth system by commenting on own behavior when he/
she fails to communicate in a clear, congruent manner.

Guide

The counselor serves as a guide toward change. As a
guide, the counselor can serve in the following ways:

1. Aids families in becoming aware of their dysfunctional
   behaviors and helps families explore alternative
   behaviors and new ways of behaving.

2. Assists families in communicating in more growth-
   enhancing ways.

3. Calls attention to facets of the family system that
   the family wants changed, when these are shown in
   behavior but are not obvious to the family.

4. Uses self, the group process, knowledge of family
   systems, and whatever techniques are in possession, to
   facilitate change and to integrate these changes into
   the family unit.

In these ways the counselor guides the family in directions
they have determined they want to go. The counselor does not
determine how they "should" change, but, rather, follows "a
step behind" their lead, assisting them in moving toward what
they have more clearly seen as desirable goals in moments of
higher consciousness, though they have difficulty maintaining
their vision.

36

These various roles of the family counselor are empha-
sized to varying degrees at different points in the counseling
process. Phase I, II, and III Charts (see pp. 59, 102, 126)
give some form indicating when the various roles are most
appropriate.

A goal to be reached in time is that the counselor will
forget the professional roles being played. Structure, methods, and theories will simply become background music to the
counselor's work and as such the counselor will be the person
who is free to be totally present with the interaction occurring at the moment. For in the last analysis, knowledge and
techniques are only two factors in the equation of the effective counseling process. Intuition, feeling, and experiencing
are factors equally vital, and these factors are limited if
the counselor is preoccupied with theory and role, taking one
away from sensitivity to the here and now.

```
* * * * * * * * * * * * * * * * * * * * * * * * * * * * * * * * * *
```

4

Section

PROCESS AND TECHNIQUE

OF

FAMILY COUNSELING

Presented With Case Example

```
* * * * * * * * * * * * * * * * * * * * * * * * * * * * * * * * * *
```

PROCESS AND TECHNIQUE OF FAMILY COUNSELING

PRESENTED WITH CASE EXAMPLE

Counseling approaches for getting the family to meet are discussed in this section, as well as adaptations of the family counseling approach with only part of the family present. Further, the counseling process itself is presented by case example with analysis of the counseling sessions. For the purposes of this writing, the assumption is made that the counselor's schedule usually allows for only a limited number of sessions with a family; therefore, process and technique in counseling are discussed on the basis of a maximum of twelve sessions. The case example illustrates counseling based on this time limit.

Techniques are offered with the precaution that the acquisition of techniques alone merely produces a technician, and family counseling is more than a technique.* A fine art develops as one gains understandings of theory and technique and the use of self and, as by experience, one finds the blending of these understandings in one's own unique style.

The choice is made in this writing to present one case example from beginning to end to provide the reader with a "feel" for both the counselor-family relationship and the process of counseling, as well as acquaint the reader with

---

*In this present age of servility to technology, the transmigration of power from theory assisted by technique, to technique and theory as equals, to technique as all powerful has occurred. In this trend, also exists an ever present danger of reductive thinking. This issue is a particularly significant one in the field of counseling where the beauty of the many dimensions of humanity must not be diminished by oversimplified formulas.

approaches to counseling used by this writer. By presenting
one case example from the beginning of counseling to the end,
the reader has the advantage of the continuity of one case.
This advantage seemed to the writer to offset the limitations
of a single case example. Obviously, by presenting only one
case the opportunity is forfeited to examine the process of
counseling in a variety of family interactions and with a
variety of family situations. Also no opportunity exists for
comparing and contrasting differing approaches to similar situations. This case offers but one model. The reader must take
from these techniques and approaches the patterns which are
appropriate to the reader's style as well as to the particular
family with whom the counseling sessions are being held.

Interventions chosen are discussed in the context of the
case material. These analyses, to the greatest extent, were
made on review and reflection by the counselor of her own
processes during the session. (During the session, of course,
such an attempt at detailed analysis is not desirable, since
the most important factor is that the counselor be fully present with the family.) By use of such detailed analysis in
the writing, however, the process of counseling is annotated
with observations, counseling principles, and the conceptual
framework on which decisions are made. This results in providing a record of the counselor's personal process within the
counseling situation. By explaining the factors considered in
making choices of interventions, the intent is that the reader
will focus on the dynamics of the decision-making process, and
that the alignment between theory and practice will be visible.

The case example which is included in this monograph, The
Williams Family, was chosen because it represents a relatively
typical counseling situation in which a child benefits from the
teacher, the counselor, and the family working together.
Furthermore, this case offers examples of numerous techniques
in counseling, because this particular family was quite responsive to the use of various techniques.

The case is divided into three phases of counseling with
eleven sessions. A discussion of each phase is followed by
case material illustrating that phase.

Through the initial telephone conversation and Session One,
the writing focuses on the process of counseling and a near
verbatim account is given. However, in the presentation of the
remaining sessions, process becomes a minor focus. Interaction
is summarized and the focus is on techniques of counseling. To
give full process interviews would exceed the material limits
prescribed for this writing.

The Beginning of Counseling, Phase I, contains three sessions in the case illustrated. Phase II, Apex of Counseling, contains six sessions in the case. Phase III contains sessions ten and eleven which comprise the Closure Phase. The next part of the book, Section V, contains "pitfalls" or difficult points in counseling and ways of dealing with them.

The term "family counseling" does not necessarily dictate that all family members be present for all counseling sessions, but rather refers to a family system assessment for which the diagnostic base of determining is who should be present in further sessions and how counseling should proceed. A family counseling approach, then, may be used in working with an individual, a partial family, or an entire family.

Preferably, the entire family will be present in the beginning of counseling in order to provide a more accurate assessment of presenting the problem in view of the family system. The presence of the entire family also is preferred at the ending of counseling in order to maximize continuation of gains which have taken place from the counseling. Exactly who is present in the medial sessions of counseling is determined by what needs are apparent in the assessment.

PREPARATIONS FOR COUNSELING

Getting The Family To Meet For The Beginning Of Counseling

Helping the family member, or members, with whom the counselor is initially speaking to understand how each member of the family is important in identifying the problem is the first effort of family counseling. Statements such as the following are useful in approaching the initial assembly of the family and serve as well to increase the family's understanding of the function of family counseling:

1. Every one of you has different opinions and ideas about the family, and all of your perceptions help the persons involved to understand. All individuals see from different angles, so pooling points of view will be an asset to gaining a fuller picture of your family.

2. When one member of the family is hurting, generally everyone in the family experiences hurt.

3. You are the only father that_____ has. Your ideas about your family are especially important.

4. Every family has its own unique personality. Understanding your family's particular personality can help you to help one another.

43

5. Each person in the family has tried many ways of making things different and if these attempts have failed, you have felt frustrated. You have tried to make things better, but you still find yourselves stuck with the problem and are unsuccessful in changing this problem. What you have tried is not working for you. Talking about this together often will help to point to new and, perhaps, more effective ways in which to try to change.

6. Many families ask for aid in understanding today's society. Because of the loss of the extended family and loss of the values that close neighborhoods once gave, we sometimes need a place and persons with whom to reflect and gain perspective.

By such statements, the counselor conveys an exploring attitude toward understanding the presented problem, and shows respect and a sense of value for each family member. The counselor conveys an attitude that problems are an indication of a blockage in growth, rather than, as is so frequently concluded, an indication that someone is "wrong" or "bad" or to blame.

Statements such as those listed are chosen to help free the family of an attitude of guilt or blame and to help the family captialize on their desire for growth. These statements are further aimed at allowing a family to come to counseling without viewing the acceptance of help as an admission of guilt or inadequacy.

Assessing The Family System

If either the family or the counselor is hesitant to involve themselves immediately in a total family assessment, preparation for the assessment may be done by initially seeing only some members of the family. This approach has the asset of facilitating a beginning relationship between the counselor and a few family members before the counselor encounters the total family group. Further, the counselor may gain some skeleton information before being encountered by a larger, more complex situation.

To be sure, this gradual preparation has its possible adverse side effects as well. Often family members will feel in collusion with the counselor against another family member, making that particular counselor-family member relationship vulnerable to misuse. This possible collusion creates simply another factor in beginning sessions with which the counselor will need to work. With awareness of this obstacle, it usually can be overcome.

Beginning Family Systems Approach With Part Of The Family Present

If, after attempting to do an assessment of the family system with the entire family, resistance to coming to a session continues to be encountered, the counselor may conclude that energies would be misdirected in further efforts toward that end. However, the desired result still might be obtained in other ways. For example, empty chairs may be used to simulate the missing family members, and their roles may be "played" by members present, still using a family approach to assessment. The counselor will in that case need to aid members present in "becoming" the absent member when they sit in his or her chair. The person who is role playing will need to feel that he or she is that person, simulated on a deeper level than is provided by mere words. To facilitate this feeling, the role player assumes the body position and gestures of the person whose role is being interpreted. The counselor asks the role player questions that might be asked if the actual person were present. For example, the following questions might be asked of the role player:

How does it feel to live in this household?

How do you feel about _____? (Other family members, particularly the one who is role playing.)

What would you like to make different in this family?

What disappoints you and pleases you in the relationship you and _____ have?

The counselor also can help the role player to answer such questions in a way that will convey the deeper feelings of the person whose role is being assumed. The counselor can assist the role player by statements such as, "Maybe you have never said these things, and maybe never would, but here it is okay to say what you really think and feel." Such a statement may aid the role player in getting in touch with the feelings that might be fantasized, or perhaps those known to be behind the absent member's usual words. Thus, by getting in touch with feelings underlying the words and by grasping, to a point, what it is like to feel like that person, the role player is substantially aided in understanding that family member, and at the same time is able to be in touch with his/her own deeper feelings toward the person.

The role-playing technique can be further used to assess the system by having the role player recall a situation of conflict and by conversing in that context with other family members.

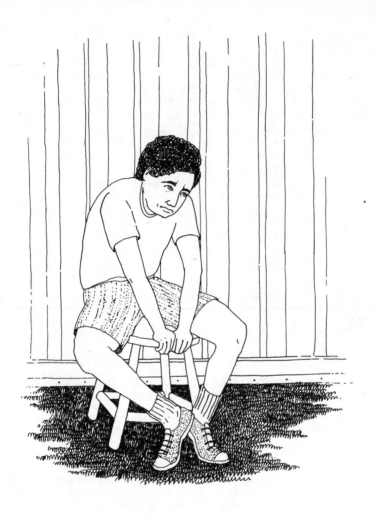

"The role player assumes the body position
and gestures of the person whose role is
being interpreted."

An Example Of Role Play With One Family Member In The Recall Of Situational Conflict

John, age 14, is in the counselor's office. The situation of conflict he recalls is when his Mom and Dad scream at him. Usually, this screaming happens at the dinner table. Susan, his 16-year-old sister, also is present. Chairs are placed as the family members sit at the dining table. The counselor assists John in becoming the member of the family with whom he feels the most conflict. He chooses Mom.

COUNSELOR: Your son says you scream at him, Mrs. C. He says he doesn't like that.

MOM (as played by John): Well, he deserves it.

COUNSELOR: When you scream at your son, how do you feel? (Counselor coaches John to say what he believes his mother really feels, though she may not say.)

MOM: Well, I don't like it either.

COUNSELOR: Sometimes when people scream, a lot is going on inside them. They may be angry at someone, or themselves, or feel sad or feel like they are not being heard or lots of things. What do you feel when you scream?

MOM: No one is listening to me.

COUNSELOR: No one? You mean Johnny isn't the only one? (Mom nods.) Who else doesn't listen?

MOM: My husband and Susan.

COUNSELOR: Say this to your son. (Counselor motions toward the empty chair that has been set up for John, in the spot where he sits at the table.)

MOM: Johnny, it isn't only you who doesn't listen to me; your Dad and Susan don't either.

COUNSELOR: Tell him, too, how you feel when no one listens.

MOM: It makes me sad.

47

COUNSELOR: (Correcting language toward more personal direction) I feel sad.

MOM: I feel sad.

After such a role-playing situation, John can identify more with what his mother feels than just with what she does. John may be able to recall what goes on inside himself when he feels he is not heard. John can see other dimensions in his mother. Perhaps now he can get in touch with how he feels about his mother being sad and share with her his feelings. So, instead of a scream being met with a protest, a feeling can be met with a feeling. This lays groundwork for John to role play a conversation with his mother as to how he might relate to his mother's feelings that are prompting her behavior, thus embarking upon a system change.

While family assessment is limited by the presence of only part of the family (as only a partial and fantasized view of the missing members is provided) role playing does offset some of the limitations. Role play frequently provides more accurate information about the system than is possible from an interview in which one family member simply talks about another. Role playing affords a more encompassing view than is possible from looking at individual dynamics alone. Role playing offers a tool for helping the members present to identify with those members whom they role play. Such a role play might be used even when the family members are all present.

After The Assessment, Who Is Seen? Why?

Once a family assessment is made, the counselor may find a further need for family counseling indicated, or may, conversely, find a need for couple, parent-child, or individual counseling. Frequently, a combination of these possibilities is utilized. The decision will evolve from both the assessment description of the particular system and the family goals for counseling. Decision making, of course, is a mutual process between family and counselor.

Advantages Of Continuing Counseling With Entire Family

Much work needing to be done with one family member or with part of the family, can be done beneficially in the presence of other family members with the following advantages:

1. Family members gain clearer understanding of and empathy for each other's struggles.

2. Confrontation with the actual struggle provides a reality check for other members who have created

mythical material for their own understanding of the
problem. By actual confrontation with areas of conflict, members face the facts of the situation.
Although this confrontation may be painful, it is
inevitably less painful than the myth, and far more
conducive to growth.

3. Family members separate themselves and the system more
   clearly and become aware of the separateness and the
   entwining.

Counter-Indications For Continuing Counseling With Entire Family

Some family situations present problems that are best
discussed with selected members of the family unit at different
times during the counseling sessions. Indications of negative
effects of entire family counseling are listed:

1. The counselor may feel overwhelmed by the number or
   intensity of problems presented. This overwhelming
   reaction could occur to the degree that efforts to cope
   with the whole family system do not seem feasible. By
   reducing the number of members involved, the areas
   involved are likewise reduced to manageable proportions.
   As more experience is gained, the counselor will find
   it easier to differentiate problem areas and work with
   overlapping segments one at a time.

2. Some family members may wish to discuss problems which
   only indirectly affect other family members, such as
   when a couple wishes to discuss details of their
   sexual life.

3. Occasionally, one or more members of a family experience such low self-esteem and such a high degree of
   inner conflict that, in the presence of others, he or
   she can feel only unrealistic blame to self, or defend
   self and blame others. This way of thinking and feeling may be so strong that, in the presence of the
   family, the person's activity of attacking and/or
   defending dominates the session. The counselor is
   unable to find any way of disrupting this destructive
   pattern. This tendency may be viewed as an indication
   of the need for individual sessions to aid the person
   in gaining personal strength so that the disruptive
   pattern within the family can be given up more easily.

4. Separate sessions for one family member may facilitate
   growth of this member's separate identity. For example,
   the adolescent's autonomy can sometimes be supported by

individual sessions, in conjunction with family
sessions, to aid the whole family in growth on the
separation-sharing continuum, the difficult task of
adolescence.

5. When most family members feel ready to work toward
   change in the family system, one family member may
   remain hesitant. Individual sessions may facilitate
   his or her readiness.

When Is The Appropriate Time To Begin Work With Part of Family? Or Recall Whole Family?

Working with part of the family is not usually recommended
until:

1. The assessment is completed.

2. Each family member sees the purpose of individual,
   couple, or parent-child counseling, in the context of
   the family system assessment.

3. Family members are willing to request a family session
   if a need for it is felt by them, or to respond to
   such a request by other members or by the counselor,
   and have agreed to return for at least one closure
   session.

Family Approach At Closure Of Counseling

If the assessment has succeeded in activating the strength
of the family toward growth, then the family has invested in
change. Regardless of who has been present in the medial
sessions of counseling, the entire counseling process will
need integration at closure with all of the family members
present. This approach maximizes the gains of counseling and
furthers the possibility of the family's continued use of
their gains after counseling.

THREE PHASES OF FAMILY COUNSELING

Family counseling tends to occur in a process which is
composed of three Phases: I, Beginning: II, Apex; and III,
Closure. These Phases apply both to the entire process of
counseling with a family and to each individual session with a
family. First, the three Phases of an individual session are
discussed. In the context of the case example beginning on
page 55 the three Phases within the entire process of counseling will be discussed. Figure 1 illustrates the three
Phases of family counseling.

The Beginning-Apex-Closure curve is the natural process of a series of counseling sessions. Likewise given an open-ended time schedule, each session of the series will normally follow this course. However, since most counselors must work by a clock, one must be aware of time (at least initially until a rhythm becomes a part of the system), in order for the three Phases to occur in a session. In a single session, generally of one and one-half hour's duration, classically the Warm-Up (Beginning) Phase will include the first ten to twenty minutes, and the Closure Phase will be ten to twenty minutes.

The Beginning Phase, Phase I, of a family counseling session is a warm-up which climbs toward the Apex and lays a foundation for the Apex. The Apex, Phase II, is more highly emotional in overtone than either of the other two phases. This Phase experiments with change. The Closure, Phase III, is a winding down and an integration of Phase II. The quality of the foundation built in Phase I determines the quality possible in Phases II and III.

The three Phases cannot be seen as completely separate processes. One Phase does not dramatically end and another begin; rather, a flow between Phases and a transition time occurs when the tasks of one Phase may blend into those of the following Phase. Phase I may evolve into Phase II, return to Phase I to build a stronger foundation, and move back to Phase II. An entire cycle of three Phases might occur with a focus in one area of conflict and be followed by a second cycle at a deeper level. With that understanding, the three Phases within a session are discussed separately. The three Phases of the entire family counseling process are discussed in the context of the Case Example, beginning on page 55.

Beginning Phase, Phase I

Phase I of one session might include:

1. Logistics. Time and place of meeting and rules related to the use of the space in the meeting room.

2. Explanation of structure for the session if one is to be used.

3. Informal conversation not directly related to counseling.

4. Report of events which have happened since the last session.

5. Review of last session.

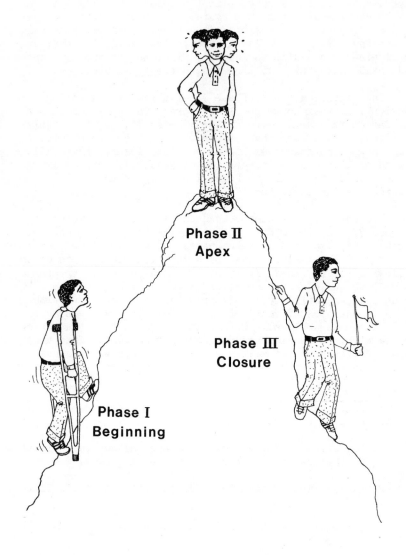

Phase II
Apex

Phase III
Closure

Phase I
Beginning

Phases in Counseling

Phase II
Apex

- increased individual
and family awareness

- process of change

Phase III
Closure

-review and integration
of learning

Phase I
Beginning

- assessment

- creation of environment for
growth

- preparation for apex phase

Figure 1. The Three Phases of Family Counseling

6. Contracting for what one wants to happen in this session.

7. Talking about fears or hesitance related to the counseling process.

This Phase offers the pattern during which the counselor and, in time, the family members attempt to build a climate conducive to the work they have to do. Each member of the group, usually privately and sometimes unconsciously, makes an evaluation of the emotional climate and tone of the session. Individuals become sensitive to how much they will trust themselves, the counselor, and one another as the session proceeds. Much of this evaluative process is done nonverbally or indirectly, though it may be brought into the open by the counselor. Focal points for the Apex of the session are determined during this period of the process.

Apex Phase, Phase II

Phase II, the Apex Phase, is a time of risking self exposure, of breaking dysfunctional family rules, and of trying new behaviors. This Phase has more highly charged emotional overtones than the other two Phases. The content may be identical to that of the Beginning Phase, but in the Apex Phase the content has an emotional charge, with the result that pieces of the puzzle of this family's life and feelings about conflicts may be openly expressed. An emotional catharsis may be experienced, as well as a deeper emotional contact with one's self and, perhaps, with each other. Communication is made clearer and individual differences might be more clearly delineated. Alternative behaviors are explored and tried.

Closure Phase, Phase III

Phase III, the Closure Phase, of a family counseling session is a time for closure and integration. The last ten to twenty minutes of a session is the time to move from the emotional level to an intellectual level. Integration is facilitated by putting experience into words. What has just happened in the session may be reviewed and summarized without limiting its impact by too narrowly categorized systems of thinking.

The Closure Phase is not a time for new material, unless one has time to deal again with a Phase I and Phase II. Closure time is essential for integration and must be protected. To deal with new material, the session would have to extend past its set time structure. Breaking the time structure, although neither impossible nor, at times, negative, is on the whole not a desirable action.

In the Closure Phase, goals for using the learning that has been gained in the sessions might be set. Contracts made between members might be reviewed and discussed in terms of how members can put them into action during the days prior to the next session.

CASE EXAMPLE

Counseling sessions with the Williams family are presented in this Section as a sometimes verbatim account of the counseling process. Each of the eleven sessions is discussed in detail in terms of techniques and processes.

The Williams family consists of the following members:

HAROLD: Age 38. Six ft. 5 in. tall. Lanky. Awkward. Former salesman, now completing degree in history with a teaching goal.

SARA: Age 36. Five ft. 7 in. tall. Housewife. Now returned to school with the hope of entering the counseling field.

MARIE: Age 11. Sixth grade. Beginning puberty. The presenting problem is her behavior.

JENNIFER: Age 9. Fourth grade.

TRACY: Age 7. Second grade.

ANNE: Age 5. Kindergarten.

The problem with which this family is concerned came to the attention of Marie's teacher as she recognized Marie's changed behavior in the classroom. Marie had begun to appear withdrawn and depressed. She had spurts of angry explosions with classmates, followed by withdrawal. She had stolen small items, such as pencils, from other children. Formerly, Marie had made good grades and was a "model student." At the time counseling began her work was very poor and she was sporadically, a management problem in the classroom.

In the teacher's subsequent routine parent conference with both Harold and Sara, the parents had reported their distress at Marie's behavior at home. They related their anger with her because she had broken a chair during a temper tantrum. She had never exhibited this kind of behavior previously. The parents said that they had tried spanking her and taking away her privileges as corrective measures, but nothing they had done or said seemed to have produced positive results. The situation had evolved to one of the parents screaming at Marie and Marie at them, with the result that Marie had developed the practice of running away. Both parents felt that Marie's behavior began to change for the worse during the preceding summer and worsened still more throughout the fall. The time now is November.

The teacher told Marie's parents that she could see their genuine concern and confusion about what to do as parents. The teacher saw that the parents wanted to help their daughter but were not sure how to do so. The teacher admitted to the parents that she, also, was puzzled and would like to have a conference with the school counselor; and she asked the parents if they would be interested in talking with the school counselor. The parents replied that they were willing to do so if it would help Marie.

The First Teacher-Counselor Conference

Marie's changed behavior in the classroom and at home was then discussed between the teacher and the school counselor. Marie's teacher shared her feelings of concern and told of the parents' willingness to meet with the counselor. The teacher furnished the counselor with all of the information given on the previous page.

In the discussion that followed between the counselor and Marie's teacher it was pointed out that Marie was evidently experiencing difficulty and the feelings behind her behavior were as yet unclear. Past records did not reveal such a problem. That the parents were distressed by their inability to reach Marie also was recognized; in fact, three family members were clearly distressed--parents and Marie. Ms. Dodson, the counselor, raised the point that possibly some changes within the family--some family crisis--might be contributing to the problem. This possibility, plus already knowing of the parents' distress and their willingness to invest in problem solving, prompted the counselor to decide to call the family and suggest a family meeting.

Further discussion with the teacher included discussion of problems the teacher had in relation to Marie's classroom behavior. The teacher had been asking Marie to tell her what was wrong. She inquired as to why Marie no longer completed her school work, but Marie did not respond to the questions asked of her. The teacher could not reach Marie when Marie was withdrawn, nor could she reach her when the child had angry explosions. In addition to asking Marie about her behavior, she had tried structuring Marie's activities and giving her special tasks in the classroom. None of these attempts had produced positive results.

In this conversation with the counselor, Marie's teacher
began to realize her own personal frustration which occurred
when she wanted to relate to Marie and had been unable to do
so. Ms. Dodson suggested that the teacher tell this to Marie.
(Here, the counselor's work with the teacher follows the principle of recognition of one's own feelings as a first step
toward making contact with another.)

Afterward, the teacher did tell Marie of her own emotional
reaction to Marie's behavior. Rather than asking such questions as, "What is wrong, Marie?" "Why don't you do your
work?", the teacher simply reported her feelings:

> "I want to understand what you are feeling, Marie.
> When I can't I feel frustrated and irritated at
> both myself and at you. I care about you, Marie,
> and I want to help you. I need you to help me
> to help you."

"Why" questions are usually unproductive. Descriptive
responses of what is, given without blame, tend to produce more
interaction and less guilt.

As Ms. Dodson unveils the family system and better understands Marie's behavior, she needs to continue to work closely
with Marie's teacher so that the teacher can gain more understanding of Marie and of the interaction between herself and
Marie as well as of the behavior of Marie toward her classmates and, consequently, can know better how to work with
Marie. The counselor will note Marie's behavior in the family
system and be attuned to possible parallels between the home
behaviors and Marie's behaviors at school. The counselor and
teacher will need to consult regularly as the counseling proceeds in order to understand the interrelationships between
Marie's behavior at home and at school, and to facilitate
change in both environments.

PHASE I - BEGINNING OF COUNSELING - IN CASE EXAMPLE

While the family in the beginning of counseling may have
much to tell the counselor about how they are perceiving their
problems, how they have tried to deal with them, and how much
frustration they have experienced, they likely do not at this
time see clearly what the problem situation is and, therefore,
cannot tell the counselor directly what is hindering their
growth. The family members can tell the outcome of the problem
(the symptom) and what they understand about its evolution.
In the manner of the telling and in their behavior, the family
members will show their distress to the counselor. But, the
counselor will need to direct and focus the session toward

gaining an assessment of the family system. Asking questions is a part of the healing process in itself, as questions can aid in gaining "new lenses"--new viewpoints--to view the distress of which the family members speak. New lenses provide a means for channeling energies in more constructive ways.

For these reasons, the counselor is more directive and active in Phase I than in either of the other Phases. This activity serves to encourage more interaction between the counselor and each family member, and allows the development of a relationship between the counselor and each person. The counselor-family member relationship contributes to a climate of trust and provides a background of support as family members take risks to confront issues with each other and to reveal themselves to each other in Phase II.

A counseling environment conducive to growth is created in Phase I by the counselor's efforts to establish a growth-enhancing system in the newly created group--that of the counselor and the family.

In the beginning of counseling, the counselor is interested in establishing the role as an aid to the family in perceiving their family system and facilitating their changes. The counselor is primarily interested in the family gaining hope for such changes as can realistically be achieved, and a belief in their own ability to make changes. They are helped in setting goals toward that end. Toward these goals, the counselor cognitively and affectively guides the family to learn about their system, giving them new lenses to use to understand their distress. The counselor conveys inner feelings of respect for the family members and their problem-solving abilities.

As the family becomes more aware of the dysfunctional elements of interaction that inhibits the changes they want, these dysfunctional rules and patterns become more difficult to abide by without conflict. If the family system is within the conscious awareness of the family members, this awareness will allow them to make change. However, at the end of Phase I, old ways of behavior have been disrupted and as yet new patterns have not been established. At this point the family may feel a great deal of anxiety. The family will need to be prepared for this possibility, and to be supported during the duration of these feelings.

The counselor's role, tasks, and hoped-for outcomes of Phase I are presented in Table 2. The pages, which follow, further illustrate the case material.

TABLE 2. PHASE I OF FAMILY COUNSELING (Beginning Phase)

Counselor's Major Roles and Nature of Interaction	Tasks	Hoped-For Outcomes
Roles 1. Teacher 2. Environmental Acclimator Nature of Interaction 1. Directs 2. Focuses 3. Is Active – People talk less with each other, more with counselor	1. Assess the System Broadly unveil system, determine its characteristics, and increase family awareness of same. 2. Create an Environment for Growth a. Establish growth-enhancing system within the system of the family counselor. b. Establish counselor role and a beginning relationship between counselor and each family member. c. Aid family in experiencing their own personal power as a group and as individuals to change. 3. Prepare for Apex Phase a. Contract for what will be goals of the Apex Phase. b. Determine who shall be present for counseling in Apex Phase.	1. Each family member views self as integral part of family problems and resolution. 2. Beginning trust in counselor. 3. Increased safety to take risks to change. 4. Hope increased in family as each member gains "new lenses" to view problems and begins to feel that they can gain tools for change. 5. Family members gain beginning idea of the process of family counseling. 6. Beginning assessment obtained and beginning goals defined. 7. System balance is disrupted as a result of dysfunctional patterns of behavior being brought into awareness.

"Beginning telephone conversations
provide the opportunity for laying
the groundwork for a family session."

Initial Telephone Contact And Process Analysis

The telephone conversation with Sara illustrates the beginning of family counseling. As much as twenty minutes might be needed for the telephone contact. Beginning telephone conversations provide the opportunity for the following:

1. Finding out who the family members are.

2. Finding out what their interaction process around the present problem is.

3. Exploring the level of awareness about the problem.

4. Laying groundwork for family sessions.

5. Beginning the tasks of Phase I.

COUNSELOR: Hello, I am Laura Dodson, the counselor at Jefferson Middle School. Are you Sara Williams?

SARA: Yes, Ms. Dodson. Marie's teacher said you might call.

COUNSELOR: You may call me Laura, and may I call you Sara?

SARA: Yes, of course.

The counselor begins by establishing names she and Sara will call each other. The use of first names is preferable when this is agreeable to the family, as it diminishes the possibility of relating to titles or positions rather than to people.

COUNSELOR: Would you tell me about your worry, Sara?

The counselor does not inquire about Marie, who is the identified problem, but asks Sara to report about herself and to talk about her own problem in relation to Marie. This is a step in the direction of establishing the growth-enhancing rule, EVERYONE CAN SPEAK FOR HIMSELF. This approach begins to unveil each family member's own strength and pain in the family.

SARA: Marie is falling down in her grades at school. At home I never know what is happening with her anymore. She is despondent, and then suddenly without any reason, she starts screaming and storms out of the house. (Talking more

61

rapidly) Why, last week in one of those temper tantrums, she jumped on the chair and broke it, and then said she was running away again. She ran out of the house, but luckily her Dad was home that day and he ran after her. He had to chase her across the park. (Laughs) Finally he caught her and brought her home. We made her stay in her room the rest of the day, but her attitude was still no better the next day.

The information Sara gives, her voice tone and laughter, and her choice of what to tell, raises issues such as the following:

1. Sara sees Marie's behavior happening without reason; that is, Sara has not been able to understand the behavior or else does not allow into her awareness what she does understand about it.

2. Her voice tone and escalation of speech indicate accelerated emotion and frustration, perhaps irritation.

3. The laughter and voice tone seem to allude to some pleasure, some secondary gain, which Sara has from Marie's behavior. Is Marie acting out something Sara would like to act out in relation to her husband? What is Sara's relationship with him? Question is further raised by Sara's pleasure at her husband's being home and chasing Marie. Something important happens in this triangle which is not explicit at this point.

4. Sara sees Harold and herself together (WE) punishing Marie. These points are raised in the counselor's mind, but exploring them further is postponed for the time being. At this point in the initial telephone conversation, the counselor is more interested in Sara's recognition of her own feelings and pain. This step is basic to the beginning of family counseling. Therefore, the counselor responds to Sara's feelings.

COUNSELOR: You sound a little amused and yet frustrated about the situation.

SARA: Yes, of course I'm frustrated. I just don't know what to do next, especially now that Marie is stealing, too.

62

COUNSELOR: Sounds like you have tried everything you know
how to try, and now you just don't know what
to do to help.

SARA: Exactly! I try, but nothing that I do works.

Now Sara begins to talk about herself and the counselor continues to encourage this by reiterating Sara's comments and
"playing back" the feelings she hears from Sara. Sara seems
now to begin to get the message that her feelings and frustra-
tions are important and worthy of being understood. They are
a part of the family situation. Beginning the unveiling of the
family system conflict so that Sara can see it and accept the
idea of family counseling is an objective of this initial
phone conversation. The counselor now moves to open another
area, which is the involvement of other family members in the
problem.

COUNSELOR: And your husband, how does he feel about the
situation?

SARA: He really loves Marie, maybe more than the
other girls. I tell him he shouldn't be
partial. He doesn't know what to do with her
either.

COUNSELOR: It must be hard on both of you to want to be
able to make things better and to feel you
don't know how and disagree about what to do.

SARA: We used to get along best with Marie of all
the kids. She won't even help at home anymore
now.

Now Sara further reports a family system problem: the feeling
on her part about her husband's feelings toward Marie. The
counselor responds by reiterating what she hears Sara say, in
a manner which contains the confrontation of the problem, yet
also contains recognition of the desire for growth. This
recognition makes the confrontation more palatable and its
effectiveness is demonstrated by Sara's response--she volun-
teers more information.

Another response that might take Sara deeper into the area
could be: "When you feel Harold is partial to Marie, how do
you feel about that?" Now the counselor pursues information to
help in understanding the presenting problem in the context of
the family.

COUNSELOR: Sounds like you feel you need more help.

SARA: Yes, I'm in school and just can't do all the work at home that I did before.

COUNSELOR: When did these changes with Marie begin?

SARA: This summer. Marie stated getting "sassy" this summer.

COUNSELOR: Do you have any ideas why things between you, Harold and Marie - that particular triangle - changed then?

SARA: Humm...no, not really - I decided to go to school in the fall. She started to develop and some of her friends teased her. I really don't know, though, what happened.

This is a beginning effort to gain information about the onset of the change-crisis (see pp. 23-25) and to begin to increase Sara's awareness that such problems can make sense partly in terms of their beginnings. The reference to the triangle reinforces the impression that in the beginning, too, more persons than Marie were involved. The counselor inquires about other family members as well.

COUNSELOR: What about your other children? Who else is in your family?

SARA: We have four girls. Jennifer is nine, Tracy is seven, and Anne is five.

COUNSELOR: Sara, how do you think that Jennifer, Tracy and Anne feel about what is happening in your family right now?

This question implies the involvement of all the family and further attempts to check out how they are involved.

SARA: Oh, they used to fight with Marie a lot, but now they try to ignore her, but I don't think they are really the problem.

Sara's response shows some reluctance to look at the broader perspective of the total family.

COUNSELOR: You know, Sara, I find it hard to say that anyone is "THE" problem. Sounds to me like all of you are trying to make things work better in your family, but there is a lot of

64

frustration. I wonder how well Jennifer,
Tracy and Anne's ignoring of Marie is working
for them, and how it makes them feel. I hear
some goals you have for yourself as a mother
are not working for you, and it sounds like
Harold is frustrated too.

Here, the counselor summarizes the family involvement, moving
toward the suggestion of a family meeting. Sara accepts the
summary.

SARA: Yes, you are right.

COUNSELOR: I often find it helpful for the whole family
to meet with me and try to work together to
understand your situation and to make things
work better.

SARA: But, I thought you were a school counselor and
worked with kids?

The proposal for the entire family to meet brings some
pulling back from Sara. Her way of understanding the problem
is being challenged. The counselor reads the protest as mild
and feels the relationship she has built with Sara to this
point can sustain the protest. She responds in an attempt to
give Sara permission to get help for herself.

COUNSELOR: (Laughs) I do work with kids but also with
adults, teachers, the principal, and whole
families, Sara. How can us big folks keep
helping kids if we don't get some help for
ourselves, too?

SARA: Do you really think it will help for all of
us to come?

COUNSELOR: I think getting a whole picture of what is
going on and what is desired gives us a good
chance to understand. Then I think we have a
start on how to make it better.

Sara is again reluctant and her reluctance is met with an
explanation of purpose but without unrealistic promises. Sara
responds positively by voluntarily revealing more information
about her distress and by focusing more on her relationship
with Harold, which before was only implied as a problem area.

SARA: Well, I guess we could sure use some help.
You know, Harold and I are arguing more and
more now, too. I'm going to school again,

and, if this house doesn't run smoothly, I
just can't get all my work done and study,
too.

COUNSELOR: Sara, would you talk to all your family about
coming in on Wednesday at 3:30 or Thursday at
4 p.m.? We will need one and one-half hours
for our meeting. You could call me back and
let me know which is the best time for you
and your family.

The choice of times helps to insure the family will talk about
coming for the session. Further, it initiates a simple
decision-making process for the family. This choice conveys
respect for the individuals and their schedules.

SARA: I don't know if I can get them to come. What
should I say to them?

COUNSELOR: Well, my idea might be to say that everyone's
point of view is important in understanding
the family and in your making it more like
each of you wish. You can tell them anything
you want from our conversation, too.

(Pause, while Sara seems to be thinking)

SARA: They all do have different ideas. The meeting
might be chaos. (Laughs) But I think I can
get them all here.

I will call you back and tell you which day is
best.

COUNSELOR: Okay, Sara. Talk to you later.

In the initial telephone contact, the counselor started
all the tasks of the Beginning Phase (see Table 2, Phase I
p. 59.) Sara has labeled the family crisis as Marie's
stealing, loss of academic achievement and running away from
home. These behaviors are seen by the counselor as possible
symptoms resulting from a family crisis which had not been
dealt with in a growth-enhancing way. Marie is not accepted by
the counselor as the problem. She focuses rather on Sara and
on the family as Sara sees it. The family system is beginning
to be unveiled and Sara has been sufficiently convinced of
family involvement to agree to the request that the family come
for the session.

The following growth-enhancing rules are put into effect
between the counselor and Sara:

Openness	It is okay to speak openly about personal feelings.
Collaboration	The counselor and family will work together to describe the family interaction which is contributing to the problem.
Opinions	Everyone in the family may have differing opinions and that is okay.
Individual	Everyone in the family is important and their contributions are valued.

> COUNSELING PRINCIPLE: The process of gathering information for the assessment and contracting can only be done effectively as a growth-enhancing system between the counselor and the family involved. This demands the establishment of growth-enhancing rules in the counselor-family system. (See Table 2, Phase I, p. 59.)

To some extent, the counselor has conveyed the idea of the counselor's role as one who helps the family to understand and change things they wish to change, as opposed to being the person who will solve Marie's problem.

In this session, the counselor has been a teacher of family systems. The counselor has activated Sara's involvement and has obtained a beginning contact for family assessment. The counselor has begun a relationship between self and Sara.

The counselor reviews the telephone conversation as she prepares for Session I. The telephone conversation has raised questions in the areas of Sara's and Harold's interaction in relation to Marie; Marie's relationship with her father and how Sara feels about that; the interrelationship of Sara attending school and Marie's behavior; Marie's onset of puberty; and how the four children relate, both in the system as a whole and with each other. The factual data on the family shows that the youngest child now has entered school. That, plus Marie's entering puberty and Sara's going to school, poses three normal family crises (see pp. 23-25). How family rules have been changed and adapted in relation to these events is pertinent data to be explored.

The Counseling Room

The room for counseling should be as functional and indestructible as possible; simple, yet attractive, so that persons present are not distracted by the arrangement of space nor concerned for the articles within the room. Movable furniture-- chairs of different sizes and shapes, a sofa, and carpet, and/or

"The counselor shakes hands with
each member of the family, moving
her face to the level of each child
to make eye contact, and introduces
herself."

large pillows or mats--allows the family to select their preferred place and does not dictate the family member's grouping
or separateness during the session. Such flexibility allows
for freer expression of body language and non-verbal communication.

Providing a table (folding one if space doesn't allow a
permanent set-up) large enough to accomodate the family and the
counselor is helpful also. The room also might afford access
to an out-of-doors area where the family and counselor may
work without interference.

A nearby bathroom and water fountain are helpful, as are
some simple toys and art materials, offering means of self-
expression. Such simple permissive space can become a pliable
tool for the family's self-expression.

The eleven sessions of the case example were conducted in
an environment similar to the one described. As you read the
sessions, try to picture the physical room environment as well
as the people and their interaction with one another.

Session One

COUNSELOR: (Shakes hands with each member of the family,
moving her face to the level of each child to
make eye contact, and introduces herself. She
gets agreement about what she and the family
will call each other, she tells them to sit
where they like. The family scatter to sit.)

COUNSELING PRINCIPLE: Body and eye contact aid
the counselor and each family member in beginning their relationship. The behavior further
conveys that, in the family counseling system,
everyone can speak for themselves, everyone can
introduce themselves, everyone is important.
The announcement that each may sit where he or
she likes introduces the idea of honoring
individual decisions and individual differences.
Immediately, then, some beginning growth-enhancing
rules are introduced.

(Sara and Harold have already moved toward
the sofa, Harold following Sara, and they sit
next to each other. Marie sits in a swivel
chair in the corner, to Sara's left. Jennifer
Tracy and Anne sit on the floor to their
father's right.)

(Pause)

COUNSELOR: Some things you all should know as we begin:
You may change your place in the room, but I
would like it if all of you will stay in the
room, or say so if you need to go out. The
toilet is just outside the door to the left
if you need it. (Pause) Now let's see, have
I told you everything I need to about our set-
up here? Oh, yes, our meeting will be
approximately one and a half hours long, is
that agreeable?

> COUNSELING PRINCIPLE: The structural set-up for
> family sessions provides boundaries within which to
> work. Making these matters explicit in the begin-
> ning frees the minds of the group of structural
> details so that counseling can proceed.

HAROLD: Sara told me about talking with you. She and
I hope we can understand our family better
and help them by coming here.

ANNE: Do you have any toys?

COUNSELOR: Just a minute, Anne. (To Harold) I want to
know more about what you hope to understand,
but first I will answer Anne's question. (To
Anne) Yes, I have these colors and these
small animals and people. (Puts materials in
a box on the floor.)

(Jennifer, Tracy and Anne begin competing for
who will have which toy. They are pushing
and talking loudly.)

COUNSELOR: This looks like something that you three have
done many times. You seem well-practiced at
it.

(Anne starts to cry and goes to sit by her
mother, who puts an arm around her to comfort
her. Jennifer and Tracy now divide the toys
under Jennifer's direction. They throw a few
things Anne's way, at Harold's request. Anne
goes to the floor by her mother's feet and
claims them. She complains that she wants a
particular toy, and her father instructs Tracy
to give it to her. Tracy does with mild
protest.)

70

"Marie is turning her swivel chair
around in circles and, most of the
time, is facing the corner."

Marie is turning her swivel chair around in
circles and, most of the time, is facing the
corner. She kicks the wall to turn herself.
Harold, in a rather loud and angry tone, tells
Marie to "Stop turning the chair and kicking
the wall and listen." Marie stops, but leaves
her chair in the position turned to the wall.
Tears come to Sara's eyes.)

Counselor's Observations And Intervention Decision. Much
interaction is occurring in this family. Most of it carries
implied, or family-coded meaning, without being explicit as to
the primary thought or feeling behind it. At this point,
almost any comment aimed past surface behavior would help to
unveil the system and begin movement toward gains in a family
assessment. For example, the counselor could (1) return to
Harold's comment, (2) focus on the interaction between the
girls, (3) focus on the interaction between Marie and Harold.
The counselor chooses not to ask for more exposure of feelings
at this point because she has not seen enough of the family
interaction to identify patterns of behavior and thus have an
idea of a significant point of focus. The relationship between
family members and counselor does not seem strong enough at
this point to justify more exposure, except perhaps, with Sara.

> COUNSELING PRINCIPLE: Unveiling the system demands
> moving into possible painful areas. It demands
> self-exposure and confrontation. Trust must first
> be built which can serve as a vessel to contain
> openness, and trust is built by developing growth-
> enhancing rules in the family-counselor system.

COUNSELOR: My, your family is busy! A lot just happened.
Is this the way things often go?

HAROLD: (In a discouraged tone) Yes, this is often
the way it goes.

(Sara cries audibly.)

COUNSELOR: What are you feeling, Sara?

SARA: (In weepy tone) I just don't understand what
is happening.

(Harold puts his arm around her and pats her.)

MARIE: "Ta, ta, ta, ta,." (Seemingly mimicking her
mother or her father's behavior toward her
mother.)

Tracy, Anne and Jennifer notice four foam
rubber mats that are 5'x4'x3" against the wall
behind them. The girls, seemingly led by
Jennifer, go to the mats, lay them down,
giggle, and sit on the pile of foam. Mother
and father seem unaware of them and unaware
of Marie.

Counselor's Observations And Intervention Decision. In
response to the counselor's question, Sara has given a thought
rather than a feeling. Through their behavior, the children
have made strong comments; however, the meaning is not at this
point quite clear. The counselor might choose as a point of
focus the behavior of the children or Sara's feeling. At
this point, however, the counselor's decision is still one of
postponing the choice of focus until the significance of the
patterns becomes visible, and until a climate of trust is
strengthened. The family is continuing the intense interaction,
and the counselor is satisfied to continue to observe and hear
this interaction.

COUNSELING PRINCIPLE: The counselor attempts to be
fully aware of family interaction and to describe
family system characteristics, and communication
patterns, as she seeks a family assessment.

HAROLD: I came here today because I am worried about
           Marie. She runs away, breaks things, and is
           really driving her mother mad. Just look at
           her now! (He glances at Marie who is turned
           facing the wall, and who continues with her
           "Ta, ta, ta," in a whisper. Then he looks at
           Sara and pats her.)

SARA: I don't know why she does these things.
           (Referring to Marie) Harold and I have talked
           and talked about it. We tried to understand
           her.

Counselor's Observations. Harold and Sara are talking
about Marie as if she weren't in the room. They have become
seemingly oblivious to what is happening around them and their
voices sound rather uninvolved as if recorded. Notice also
the choice of words: Sara says they have talked about "it,"
an impersonal reference to Marie. When two family members are
involved with each other about a third, the indirect communication is the most obvious dysfunctional element. Family
collusion is seen: "Let's you and I talk about him." At some
point this collusion will have to be given attention. At the
moment, Harold is continuing his story with some pressure of
speech. The counselor is responding to what seems to be

73

Harold's need to be heard. In her judgment, Harold does not appear ready for intervention.

> (Harold relates the story of the chair inci-
> dent (p. 62) and as he does so, Marie con-
> tinues her "Ta, ta." Jennifer and Anne are
> now burying Tracy between the mats and sit-
> ting atop the pile. All three are giggling.)

Counselor's Observations. Enough interaction has emerged to reveal a possible pattern of behavior and to suggest the operation of such dysfunctional rules as the following:

1. Father comforts mother if mother feels upset about Marie.

2. Father and mother talk about Marie.

3. Children must compete with intensity and with fre-
quency. (Exactly what goes into the need to compete is yet unclear, but that the children enter into action which is seemingly related to parents' behavior, looks to be a pattern.)

4. Sara and Harold talk, the girls act.

> COUNSELING PRINCIPLE: Rigid rules are indicated by behaviors which are repeated regularly in response to a "cue." The counselor may assume that the more rigid the rule, the greater the need for it.

Intervention Decision. In the counselor's judgment, the trust relationship between herself and Harold seems to have grown, perhaps more nonverbally than verbally, and the coun-selor feels intervention now can be sustained. This inter-vention could not be done with Marie or any of the other children as a trust relationship between them and the counselor is not yet present. The counselor's choice is to focus on Harold's indirect communication and, as she does, the session moves from Phase I into Phase II.

> COUNSELING PRINCIPLE: When one or more family members have moved into a relationship with the counselor and appear to have more trust and comfort in delving more deeply into conflict areas, the counselor, by moving ahead with this person, may demonstrate to other family members that it is safe to expose feelings and talk about issues in the family. The counselor attempts to judge readiness of individuals and does not ask for exposure beyond

74

the readiness that seems present. Relationship
between counselor and individual is a base to this
readiness.

COUNSELOR: (To Harold) Would you talk to Marie about
these things?

(He hesitates and seems unable to grasp the
request at a meaningful level. The request is
repeated simply.)

HAROLD: (To Marie) Honey, we want to help you. Your
mother is upset.

COUNSELOR: (To Harold) I believe you want to help, but
notice what just happened, Harold. Sara is
upset with Marie, and then you try to help
Marie for the purpose of helping Sara.

HAROLD: (Thoughtful and seeming a bit confused.)
Maybe so.

Counselor's Observations. Harold has not yet given a
whole communication message to Marie. He inserts Sara into
their communications. This insertion is a clear indication
that more work needs to be done with Harold before Marie will
be able to receive a clear message, and thus have the opportunity to make a clear response.

(Marie has stopped her "Ta, ta, ta," and has
turned her chair around and is facing her
father and listening.)

COUNSELING PRINCIPLE: The degree of personal awareness determines the quality of communication and
the quality of actions or outcomes.

COUNSELOR: (To Marie) Marie, what do you think?

(Marie looks at the counselor but does not
verbally respond.)

COUNSELOR: I noticed your "Ta, ta, ta," as you twirled
yourself in the chair. How do you feel toward
your Mom and Dad right now?

MARIE: Oh, Mom always cries.

HAROLD: (To Sara) Maybe she is just growing up dear.
I'm sure she will be okay.

COUNSELOR: I notice again, Harold, that you talk to Sara

about Marie. I wonder what would happen if you didn't get caught in a three-way thing . . . know what I mean?

HAROLD: I am just trying to help . . .

COUNSELOR: Yes, I know. I believe you care about both Sara and Marie, and all your family, and that you want to help. You said earlier that you wanted to understand more, and I believe you do. I want to try to help you to understand as I see things that might be in your way.

> COUNSELING PRINCIPLE: The effective counselor sees the direction in which a family member, or the group, is moving and facilitates their movement by following their lead. The counselor, so to speak, stays "a half step behind;" that is, the counselor hears the direction the person wants to go and facilitates movement in that direction by following the lead and helping to remain on the edge of the desire, yet reluctance, to change.

Intervention Decision. In the preceding dialogue, the counselor has opted for a gentle confrontation with Harold. This is part of the second phase of Session I, but also must be viewed as the first phase of the entire counseling process and, therefore, a time of more intellectual awareness than of emotional awareness.

(Now the three younger girls have opened the sliding glass door leading outside. It seems that Jennifer has gotten Tracy to ask the counselor if they can go outside. Once again, father and mother seem oblivious to what the children are doing. They are talking with each other again about what is wrong with Marie. Sara still has tears.)

COUNSELOR: (To Jennifer, Tracy and Anne, who are standing around her) How do you feel about your mother crying and your dad comforting her just now?

TRACY: Oh, she always cries. Can we go outside?

(The counselor gives permission to Tracy, Jennifer and Anne to go out, and Marie immediately gets up and joins them. All four girls exit. Mother and Father continue their talk about Marie, and Sara continues to weep quietly and wipe her tears.)

Counselor's Observations. The counselor has been distracted from her initial intention of delving more into direct
~~communication between Harold and Marie.~~ ~~Sara and Harold~~
resumed their talk as the girls exited. The family system has
avoided the intervention that the counselor had almost made.
The counselor now wonders how rigid the family system is and if
it will allow intervention in these behaviors at this time.
Another route may need to be taken to facilitate intervention.

Intervention Decision. The counselor is aware of her
feeling of boredom with the parent's conversation. She is
aware that more energy is present in the children's interaction
than the parents; and, experiencing a personal preference
toward action rather than the parents talking about Marie, she
is drawn to the children.

> COUNSELING PRINCIPLE: The counselor pays attention
> to personal feeling responses and honors them within
> the counseling process.

(The counselor goes to the door and looks out
at the children. All the girls are running
around the yard energetically. Marie suggests
that they play leap-frog. Tracy first responds "Yes" and Jennifer and Anne push for
position of first in line for the game. The
game begins. Inside, mother is continuing
to cry and father is saying, "Things will be
okay.")

COUNSELOR: (To Sara and Harold) I don't really understand what is happening in your family just
yet, so I am following along with what is
going on for now. I'm going out to be with
the girls for a while. You may come if you
like.

(Sara immediately stops crying and she and
Harold both look at the counselor in surprise.
They get up and come to the door where she
is standing. Sara laughs at what she sees.
(The children playing leapfrog.) The counselor opens the door to go out and Sara
laughs.)

(It sounds like a laugh of some puzzlement
and some pleasure as well. Harold looks at
his wife as if to be certain she is okay.
They go outside. The children stop their
game in surprise.)

77

Counselor's Observations. The counselor's earlier attempt to disrupt family patterns of behavior by directing others toward changed behavior was not successful. Now, the counselor's direct involvement of herself in the system, following intuitive responses to it, is effective. The dysfunctional rules which have been outlined previously have been disrupted. The question in the counselor's mind is which feelings are protected by these rules. Perhaps, now that the rules have been broken, protected feelings will emerge.

> COUNSELING PRINCIPLE: By increasing the family's awareness of dysfunctional behaviors, the counselor begins to disrupt patterns, and the equilibrium of the family may be upset temporarily by the counseling process (See Table II, Phase I p. 59, Hoped for Outcomes).

(The counselor announces that she would like to play with the girls. Marie laughs. Jennifer exclaims: "You want to play!" There is general pleasure, surprise and laughter among the girls. The counselor bends down as the children are doing. Jennifer instructs her father to bend down, too, like a frog. When he does, Marie quickly jumps over him, giggling. Everyone gets into the game and there is apparent pleasure for all and several moments of intense, exhausting play. Father falls down on the ground and all four children pile on top of him. Sara moves toward the counselor, seated on the ground, and heaves a sigh. The game subsides.)

COUNSELOR: You know, I was really surprised at you, Sara, how quickly you stopped crying and came out to play.

SARA: It is fun to play with the children. I don't do that very often.

COUNSELOR: Would you like to do it more?

SARA: Yes, I would. I miss them.

COUNSELOR: It was fun, wasn't it? I liked playing with your family, too. You all have much warmth and caring for each other that sometimes gets lost within each of you with all the words.

(Harold is now sitting up with a glowing look on his face, turned toward Sara and the

78

"You all have much warmth and
caring for each other that
sometimes gets lost within
each of you because of all
the words."

counselor. Marie sits behind him, facing away
from the family, and slightly touching her
Father's back. The other girls sit in a
circle with Sara and the counselor. Anne is
touching her Mother, Jennifer is between Anne
and her Father, Tracy is next to her Father,
her head against his leg.)

HAROLD: We used to play a lot. Sara and I just lived
              to have our kids and have a lot of fun with
              them.

              (Tracy and Jennifer snuggle closer to their
              Father.)

COUNSELOR: (Teasingly) You have a lot of women who want
              to be close to you. You're the only guy with
              such a lovely group of females!

HAROLD: (Looking slightly embarrassed but proud)
              "Yeah," Me and all my girls.

> COUNSELING PRINCIPLE: Nonverbal behavior is fre-
> quently more significant than spoken words, but is
> to be observed and checked out before clear inter-
> pretation of meaning is made.

Counselor's Observations and Intervention Decision. The
area just opened with Harold, if explored, might give pertinent
information; for example, Harold's feelings about his family
and the competitive situation with the girls might be better
understood. However, the end of the session is near and,
therefore, this area is not pursued. The moment described had
impressed the counselor with Harold's position as the only
male and with the response of his daughters toward him. So she
chose to provoke an expression of his feelings on the matter.

> COUNSELING PRINCIPLE: Phase II of the session
> offers an emotionally corrective experience. In
> Phase III intellectual integration is more important
> than further emotional interaction (see p. 54).

COUNSELOR: I am wondering what stops the family from
              playing more together lately. You all seem
              hungry for it.

MARIE: He is never home now ....

COUNSELOR: Your dad is gone a lot?

MARIE: Yup, and I miss him.

COUNSELOR: (Mainly to Harold and Sara) I see the two of
you puzzling to understand what is happening
in your family. I am working with you to
discover the pieces to the puzzle. I know
you are both in school now, and that your
family has made more changes this fall with
Anne going to school for the first time, and
with Marie growing up. These things can make
a lot of stress. (Harold and Sara express
agreement.) Also, Tracy, Jennifer, and Anne,
you gals seem to be putting a lot of energy
into competing. These are some of the pieces
that we will want to understand better. (Met
with nods and giggles.) Let's keep looking
for more pieces.

(A discussion follows of the memories of times
when the family played together. The counselor reiterates the difficulty between
Harold, Sara and Marie in the session. With
questions and prompting, she aids the family
in recalling this and all the family reaffirms
the discomfort. Jennifer, echoed by Anne,
says she does not want to be like Marie. The
counselor does not investigate the comment
due to the time factor. She simply comments
that all of us are unique and she would hope
none of us would try to be just like another.
The counselor returns to earlier behavior
that she thinks needs integration before the
session ends.)

COUNSELOR: I am puzzled by your tears, Sara. Tears can
mean a lot of things, and I am not sure what
yours mean.

SARA: (Seems to invest in the question.) I don't
know.

Intervention Decision. The counselor moves to a more
emotional experience which is properly part of Phase II, but
the counselor decides that brief work can be done and this
important piece merits digression in the session.

COUNSELOR: Sara, would you give your tears a voice and
let them say what they meant? Be your tears.

SARA: (After some encouragement) I feel helpless
and hopeless. Maybe that's about Marie.

81

COUNSELOR: I can imagine it is very hard for you to feel helpless and hopeless. You're a very able woman.

SARA: Yes. (Starts to weep).

Counselor's Observations. Sara's expression of her feelings is a helpful step in the counseling process. Being more clearly aware of what the hopelessness is about and seeking to alleviate or live with it (as is appropriate) is the next step. Another possible dysfunctional family rule has been exposed: "Don't ask directly that your needs be met."

COUNSELOR: Sara, I don't know exactly what you are feeling helpless and hopeless about. I think it is more than Marie's behavior, but this is something I think we can better understand together. I see Harold trying to help you with your feelings, yet it seems to me that his efforts to help do not change your feeling (Sara shakes her head "no") I would like to puzzle with you about what is causing your pain and how we can make things better. It may be that by doing this we will have one more piece for understanding the pain in the family. (Sara stops crying and seems to be listening intently, as does Harold, who now has an arm around Tracy, and is leaning back against Marie. All the family seems to be listening) It is time for us to stop today. I suggest we meet again soon and continue. What do you think?

(There is discussion about coming back. Tracy says she wants to come and play some more. Harold questions if the counseling process will help Marie. He is reassured that understanding the family provides a baseline from which to help. It is suggested that in the coming week Harold put to use the direct method of communication with Marie. All family members agree to come again. Approximately ten to twelve sessions with the family are offered by the counselor. The session ends.)

COUNSELING PRINCIPLES: (1) In the first phase of counseling, the counselor must determine if this family possibly can be helped and if the family is willing to contract with the counselor. (2) If the approximate number of sessions must be predetermined, the counselor has the responsibility of so informing the family early in counseling. This knowledge in itself tends to help regulate the depth of the counseling process and allows time for closure.

Review of Session One

Analysis of the Session by Sociogram.* During the foregoing session this family has enacted four distinct sociograms. Because the interactions and dynamics of any family session are so numerous and frequently complex, a reflective tool such as the sociogram allows the counselor, in retrospect, to consider the dynamics involved from a graphic and visual perspective.

In the first part of the session Sara and Harold are inseparable. The three younger children are distant from the parents and from Marie. Marie separates herself from the rest of the family. The parents tend to react to the children as if they comprise a unit. The daughters tend to behave as if they were a unit. Marie takes the role of "flag-waver." Her activity with the swivel chair and her mimicking seem to comment on the whole family's dysfunctional behavior.

Sociogram I:

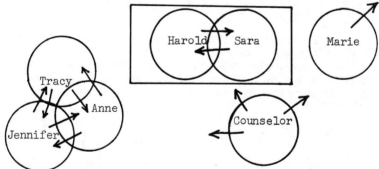

In Sociogram I is shown interaction during the first part of Session one. No specific form exists for drawing a sociogram, the form simply should be the one that aids the particular counselor in visualizing the body communication. The progression of interaction in this interview as in Sociogram II shows movement toward a more growth-enhancing system.

---

*A sociogram is a graphic representation of the configuration of members of a group indicating their sociometric relationship to each other (Moreno, 1953).

Sociogram II:

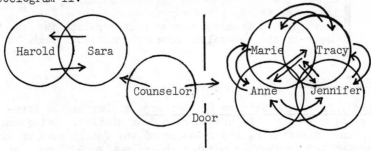

A third configuration emerges as the parents and counselor exit and engage in the game. Body contact of everyone occurs in this game. Nonverbally, the family seems to make very complete and satisfying contact and dysfunctional rules are broken. The circles are not named as constant motion occurred.

Sociogram III:

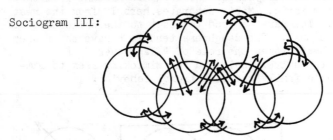

After the play, a fourth configuration or sociogram emerges. Sara voluntarily moves away from the family toward the counselor. This, and subsequent behaviors, might indicate some flexibility in her seeming need to have Harold's continual support. Marie, Jennifer and Tracy move closer to their father; Anne to her mother.

Sociogram IV:

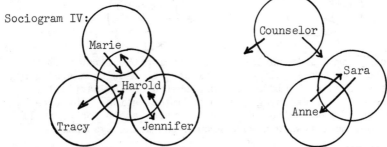

Sociogram IV reflects body language more congruent with the underlying feelings. The earlier tension was reflected in the seating arrangement of Sociogram I, which was illustrative of dysfunctional rules in the family. Marie, and possibly Jennifer and Tracy, wish to reach their father, and Anne her mother. What stops the flow of contact? This question, to be further explored, emerges more clearly by a series of sociogram views of the family.

Active Listening. Active listening refers to the techniques of listening and reflecting, and of questioning the person who is speaking in order to assist him or her in focusing and clarifying thoughts and feelings. This technique helps the speaker and the counselor to hear fully what is being said and to identify the problem. Implicit in this technique is respect for the people with whom the counselor is working, belief that what the family members are experiencing can be communicated sufficiently to focus the problem, and that in clarifying the problems the persons frequently find their own solutions.

With an attentive attitude on the part of the counselor, with nods, with questions that might clarify the communication, and observations that might prompt further clarification, the counselor works toward the simple goal of helping the people to clarify for themselves the problem at hand. The counselor does not offer solutions, criticism, or comment other than paraphrasing what the person is saying. Even this paraphrasing is offered for the family members verification as the counselor does not imply that what she sees or hears is, in fact, what they experience.

This approach is helpful when the family member seems to be giving information with obvious emotional importance to the person, which is too partial, without effect or focus, or not clearly expressed. The problem is not clearly identified, thus resolution is ineffective. This approach is used in the initial telephone conversation on p. 61. On pp. 89-91 in Session Two, further examples of active listening are provided.

Voice Technique. The specific technique used with Sara in relation to her tears is called the voice technique. Talking about a feeling sometimes gives emotional distance from it and produces a discrepancy between the feeling and the words used to describe it. In asking Sara, "What do your tears mean?" Sara is invited to think about meaning. This focus may be difficult for a person not in touch with the feeling generating the tears. By asking Sara to give a voice to the tears, the counselor provides an opportunity for experiencing the feelings as they happen. This technique is effective especially when a discrepancy exists between the content of what is being said and one's body messages.

Confrontation. When a graphic example of dysfunctional behavior has just occurred, direct feedback, which is called here "confrontation," often is effective. The counselor con-

85

fronts Harold about the matter of speaking with Sara about
Marie (pp. 75-76). This approach is a direct move toward and
sometimes a move past the edge of resistance. Even if the person who is confronted rejects the confrontation, the issue is
at least in the open, and the counselor can then assess what
factors prevent the recognition or acknowledgement of it.
Confrontations, however, must be made with an effort to
clearly and directly impart information, in an attitude of
caring, and never with an ulterior motive of attack or expression of anger or "oneupsmanship."

Use of Self. The use of self is the essence of the
counseling process and only with hesitation is it here
approached as a technique. However, the technique may be beneficially discussed in order to illustrate the specific usage
during the session just described. The counselor's feeling
response to the family members is a basic cue to the counselor
in interacting with the family. Knowing oneself and one's
own family system provides a safeguard to assist the counselor
in responding to the moment with the family rather than to a
projection of one's personal conflicts. The counselor does
not always "think through" personal reactions during the
session to the point of being able to verbalize what he/she
is doing and why. Usually it is on reflection that the counselor can see more clearly his/her emotional response and
subsequent behavior with the family.

In the first session with the family, the counselor felt
the pain of the indirect communication between Harold and Marie
and responded with confrontation. The counselor felt the
separateness of the younger children and was aware of their
relegation to a unit. The counselor, too, felt the children's
desires to play outside as a need greater than that of a
whimsical wish for fun. A trap-like repetition of pain seemed
to occur in this family which the counselor personally was
beginning to experience as distress and sadness. Certain that
personal reaction was strongly related to the current experience, the counselor allowed the feeling to move her toward
the children and to join them in their play. When the counselor perceived the abruptness of Sara's transition from tears
to laughter, the counselor was surprised and shared the feeling.
Then later, feeling the presence of one man in the group and
the affection flowing toward him from his family, the counselor
commented on that feeling.

Other feelings the counselor experienced were not
expressed. These feelings were no less felt, no less valid;
but for various reasons verbally expressing them at the time
did not seem appropriate. However, the counselor recognized
at the same time the likelihood that the unexpressed feelings

were nonverbally influencing the counseling process. Specifically, these feelings were as follows:

1. Sadness for Marie in the corner.

2. Pleasure with Marie in reaching her father during the game.

3. Distress for Sara in relation to her need to cling to Harold early in the session.

4. Empathy for the sincere attempts of this family to work out their problems.

Preparation for Session Two

The initial phone call with Sara Williams about Session One was presented with the process of family counseling as the main focus and with techniques summarized. From this point on, the remaining sessions are presented with only a summary of the process, to offer a contextual framework, and with the examples of techniques involved as the major focus.

By checking the Tasks and Hoped-For Outcomes columns in Table 2, Phase I (p. 59) the counselor gains a clearer picture of what further sessions in this Phase will need to entail. Review of the Characteristics of a Family System (pp. 14-21) can further assist the counselor in knowing where to focus. The counselor determines that

1. numerous facts are needed as the assessment continues;

2. relationships between family and counselor need to be strengthened;

3. contracts will need to be made for the continuation of counseling.

The counselor has determined that the family system has sufficient flexibility to make the changes they seem to want. This flexibility is indicated in the first session by the family's ability to respond to interventions and to allow the system rules to be altered. For these reasons, the counselor selected the Structured Interview Technique.

The Structured Interview Technique. The Structured Interview Technique was first devised by Watzlawick (1966) for the purpose of research with families. A modification of his technique was used with the Williams family and, indeed, this technique lends itself to further adaption to suit a counselor's specific needs for any particular family. The Struc-

87

tured Interview helps the counselor focus on information necessary for unveiling the family system, with the advantage of shortening the time needed to gain such information. This technique also provided an opportunity for the beginning of contracting with each family member. Such planned activity is more effective when trust relationships are built sufficiently to sustain the imposition of a structure.

Mention should be made that any structured session has the disadvantage of interrupting the natural flow of interaction, thus diminishing the spontaneous flow and the type of learning that can evolve from following that flow.

Session Two--Structured Interview Technique

Had the Williams family arrived at Session Two with topics in mind which would lead in a direction not amenable to the Structured Interview, then the decision to use this technique would have been voided or postponed. However, this was not the case; the family entered the session with greater ease and more flexibility than had been evidenced in the first session. Harold reported that more direct communication had taken place between himself and Marie. Marie did not resume her position in the corner. After this brief "warm up," the Structured Interview Technique was introduced to the family as a series of games with the purpose of helping all of the individuals to grasp an understanding of the family and to focus on what the family members wanted to make different in their relationships.

The Structure was arranged in four parts. The first task related to what each member would change in the family if change were in their exclusive power to do. This question is designed to gain a view of how each member of the family perceives the main problem in the family. It affords the opportunity for the counselor to talk one at a time with family members, making the beginning of a contract between the counselor and that family member as to what they want for themselves from the session. This dialogue facilitates each person's involvement in the problem/solution process. It is aimed at the individual's feelings and at involvement of that individual's positive energy in the family stress.

> COUNSELING PRINCIPLE: A goal of Phase I is that each family member will view self as an integral and important part of the family problems and solutions. (See Table II, Phase I--Hoped-For Outcomes, p. 59.)

A second task was a decision-making process between various family members to gain further understanding of relationships within the family and their current decision-making processes.

88

> COUNSELING PRINCIPLE: Revealing the decision-
> making process can show roles that family members
> play.

A third task was recounting some elements of family history to provide a contextual perspective on the current problems the family was experiencing.

> COUNSELING PRINCIPLE: Family members will tend to
> reveal only as much information as is comfortable
> for them to reveal. In questioning further, the
> counselor should be aware of the strength of the
> relationship that has been built between herself
> and the family member, the receptivity of the family
> to hear the information and the degree of hesitancy
> in revealing it. The counselor must attempt always
> to operate just on the edge of resistance and not
> push the family too far nor fail to probe suffi-
> ciently.

A last task was to give opportunity for expression of
positive and negative feelings within the family as well as
expression of differences, and to reveal further the relationships within the family.

> COUNSELING PRINCIPLE: The acceptance of individual
> differences and of positive and negative feelings
> toward the same person contributes to the creation
> of a growth-enhancing environment.

Structured Interview with the Williams Family

Task One. Each family member was asked individually in
the presence of the group, "If you had a magic wand and could
make one thing in this family different that would help you,
what would you change?"

To illustrate how one can deal with the responses to this
question and keep the desired focus, the following interaction
between Marie and the counselor is presented:

MARIE: She (Mother) always screams at me. I'd like
            her to stop.

COUNSELOR: And how do you feel when your mother screams
            at you?

MARIE: I get mad.

COUNSELOR: When someone feels mad, usually they feel some other things before they feel the mad feeling. What do you feel as you hear your mother screaming at you?

MARIE: I feel like hitting back, I feel like running away.

COUNSELOR: And before you feel like hitting back or running away what do you feel?

(There is a pause and no response. The counselor continues.)

COUNSELOR: Sometimes, when I feel someone is screaming at me, I feel sad or feel like crying, and sometimes I feel ashamed if I don't like me for what I have done. Do you ever feel those ways?

MARIE: (Reluctantly) Sometimes.

COUNSELOR: Which one?

MARIE: Sad.

COUNSELOR: When your mother screams you feel sadness inside you. Then after that, you get mad, right?

MARIE: Uh-huh.

COUNSELOR: What is this sad feeling like?

MARIE: I don't know.

COUNSELOR: Right now you are not sad, Marie, but could you imagine yourself being sad?

(Marie imagines her mother telling her again that she has been bad, that she didn't help her (Mother) today. She begins to be more in touch with the feeling she has labeled "sad." She is asked to make her body look like the sad Marie, and she hangs her head and shoulders, then she is asked to tell what it is like to be sad.)

MARIE: I am the worst kid here. She thinks . . . (She looks at her Mother and the anger takes over.)

> (The counselor encourages Marie to stay with the feeling of sadness just now, and Marie continues.)

MARIE: My mother used to like me best and now she doesn't like me.

COUNSELOR: (Actively listening) You don't feel your mother likes you anymore. And would it be fair to say that you sometimes don't like yourself as much as you used to?

> Conceptual Framework: Another person's negative feeling toward us is not likely to affect us deeply unless reinforced by our own similar feelings, and it is only the latter that the individual has the power to change. By changing it, however, frequently self-presentation is changed, in turn effecting the responses of the other.

At first it was difficult for Marie to accept the idea of self-dislike, and so it was presented to her in another way: That there are parts of herself which she does not like. Marie responded that she did not like the fact that she was lonely, that she felt ugly, and a lot of people did not like her. A contract was made then that Marie wanted help with liking herself better as the sessions progressed, and that she, specifically, would like help with feeling better about the way she looked and about relieving the feeling of loneliness. In addition she wanted help to improve the relationship between herself and her mother. She expressed to her mother a wish that her mother would like her. Elaboration on that dialogue was postponed in order to first allow the focus on self to be experienced. To have her mother hear Marie's feelings without Mother having to react to them was enough at this time.

Task Two. "By pretending that you will be together one evening or weekend without the other family members present, plan where you will be and what you will do for the time you will spend together. Two minutes are allowed for the decision-making process." The counselor stepped back from the group and watched the interaction process.

The counselor used this technique with these four combinations of the Williams family members and for these purposes: (1) the four girls, to observe change or similarity of competition between the four children without the parents present; (2) the parents, to observe the relationship between Sara and Harold; (3) Marie and her father, to observe the relationship between Marie and her father when alone, thus differentiate the effect of other family members on their interaction; and, (4) the parents and Tracy and Jennifer, to observe the parents with the two middle children, (whose separate identities seemed less defined than those of the other children) with particular regard for their identities in relation to their parents when fewer children were present.

All of the previous issues related to assessment of the family system and were raised in the first session. The results of the activity were as follows: (1) Competition between the four girls was not lessened to a significant degree without the parents present. This fact was taken by the counselor as further indication of a total family theme of the need to compete. (2) Harold and Sara were able to take advantage of the suggestion that they plan an activity for the two of them, and to jointly involve themselves in the planning. They stated that doing this task brought back memories of quite some time past when they did plan time for the two of them to spend alone. (3) Marie and her father seemed to become more aware of their mutual wish to be closer and their mutual hesitancy to do so, which was evident with or without the presence of other family members. (4) Tracy and Jennifer did emerge as separate individuals to a greater degree when their sisters were not present, indicating flexibility in this facet of the system. Individuality in each family member seemingly was enhanced when some of the strong need to compete diminished. These factors indicated to the counselor what direct suggestions might be made to the family for helping them break some of the dysfunctional and implied rules.

Task Three. This task was taken in three parts. Each part was completed with the entire family present.

First part, the parents were asked to relate how--out of all the people in the world--they chose each other. They were asked to describe how they met, what had attracted them to each other, what kind of things they had hoped for in marriage, and to tell about the early years of the marriage. (In this manner the beginning of the family system may be unveiled, and both the family and counselor may discover in the foundation some myths and strengths which possibly continue to influence behavior.)

Second part, Sara was asked to talk about herself when she was Marie's age, particularly in relation to her movement from childhood to adolescence. (The similarity of Sara's and Marie's problems was recognized by the family and by the counselor.)

Third part, Harold was asked about his experience in entering adolescence. Harold revealed his difficulties at that stage of his life.

The Williams were asked to focus historically on the family, with even greater focus on the foundations which were most likely to be related to the current crisis. Such focus, in addition to revealing pertinent information, gives a broader perspective to the family's current crisis. Then, too, by hearing about their parents' childhoods and marriage, children often are able to gain information that enables them to see their parents as individuals, rather than merely as people in the role of parents.

This part in the third task seemed to affirm that Harold and Sara had focused on the development of a family system that included young children, (four of them coming rather rapidly into their lives soon after marriage), and that they had developed a system that was more operational when the children were younger. It became clear that the difficulty of changing the system as the children grew older was complicated by the parents' own self-images and the difficulties they each had experienced in entering their own adolescence.

Task Four. Members were asked to sit in a circle. Each was given a piece of paper on which to write the thing they liked most about the person to their right (or left), as well as the thing they liked least about that same person. The counselor then collected the papers without revealing the content to anyone.

The counselor reworded the collected statements which applied solely to one member, such as, "she rolls my hair," so that the statements read, "she helps me." The meaning of the statement was retained but broadened, so that its meaning might apply to any member of the family rather than to one individual member. (The counselor may, where it is felt helpful for purposes of inclusion of other members, add statements of personal choice to expand the variety of areas covered, but in such case, the counselor would inform the family of what is being done.) When statements such as "she helps me" were read aloud by the counselor, the family was asked to vote for the person in the family to whom, in their opinion, the statement seemed most related. The family voted verbally, while the counselor recorded the voting on a form such as follows:

COMMENT	HAROLD	SARA	M	J	T	A
This person helps me						
This person listens to me						
This person has a hot temper						
This person knows my moods						
This person is busy and ignores me						

Under each person's name, the counselor wrote the name of the person for whom they had voted in response to each question.

This exercise aids in exposing alliances, scapegoating, or a feeling of freedom of response among the family members. It further helps to create growth-enhancing rules in the family-counselor system by accepting both negative and positive feelings, by recognizing that both feelings may exist about the same person, and by creating opportunity for and acceptance of a difference of ideas among different family members. Some unique characteristics of individuals then may indeed begin to be identified.

In the fourth task of the interview, Marie demonstrated a desire to check with her mother, by glances, before giving a positive response toward her father. While Sara gave no indication of either permission or reassurance, she did not interfere. Tracy and Jennifer seemed to emerge as a twosome, responding identically on most issues. Sometimes they discussed between them how they would vote and their discussions were filled with laughter and apparent attempts to use their responses to tease, or offer support to, other family members. Anne drew close alliances to her mother. There was a notable absence of any ability on the part of the family to move close to various members and away, and then close to another member. On the contrary, discomfort with expression of positive feeling seemed to be present.

At the conclusion of Task Four, the Closure Phase of the interview, a discussion followed. This discussion facilitated some integration of material and feelings generated in the session, Ms. Dodson asked the family what new information had

94

been learned about themselves, about the other family members, and about the family as a whole. The counselor gave her observations and the family reacted to them.

With the Williams, some decisions were made for working toward modifying selective behaviors during the coming week. Harold and Sara decided to spend time together without the children, perhaps an afternoon or an evening. Some time for each of the parents to spend alone with each child was set as a goal. Harold asked Marie if he could do some activity with her that coming week, and they decided to do her homework together one evening.

The family seemed to have left the interview with higher energy and relatedness to each other and more of a hope for change. The structured exercises apparently had contributed a lighter, more playful manner in which to learn about themselves and led, therefore, to a more willing acceptance of what had been learned.

The family took more risks to reveal themselves and their system in areas they seemed to want changed, indicating movement toward a more growth-enhancing system. Each family member seemed to be gaining understanding of the process of counseling and to be making more investment in change (see "Hoped-For Outcomes" Table 2, Phase 1, p. 59, and Growth-Enhancing Rules, pp. 16-19).

Counselor's Review And Assessment Of The Williams Family By Systems Characteristics

In reviewing Table 2, Phase I, p. 59, and the Conceptual Framework for Family Counseling (Section 2, pp. 13-27) in the light of these initial contacts, the counselor determined that sufficient information has been gathered about the family to engage in contracting for continued counseling.

The counselor has made the following assessment: The presenting problem of Marie's stealing, running away, being withdrawn, having temper tantrums, and falling down in her grades, seemed to be the symptomatic outcome of several interrelated factors in the family system. These factors were as follows:

1. Normal Family Life Crises (see pp. 23-25)

Marie is entering adolescence. Simultaneously, her youngest sister, Anne, is going to school for the first time. Sara is relinquishing her mothering role to an extent and is entering school. Hence, three normal family-life crises are occuring simultaneously.

95

2. Dysfunctional Rules (see pp. 15-19)

The following dysfunctional rules seem to have developed in the family system:

a. Sexual feeling is to be diverted or ignored but certainly is not to be an expressed or recognized part of life. This rule is revealed in the parents' talking about their transition to adolescence and in their relating to Marie in the area of her sexual development.

b. Asking directly for love needs, for needs of recognition, and for affirmation of self, is not acceptable. Instead, competition is the norm mode for attempting to meet these needs. Recently the balance of the system has been disrupted by modes of behavior to meet these needs that are less socially acceptable, such as temper tantrums and stealing.

c. Communication between Marie and her father is mostly achieved dysfunctionally, by running away, having temper tantrums, or, in an indirect pattern, through mother. Mother and father can talk about Marie, but to talk directly with her, or (especially) for father to talk directly to her, did not happen. Also, she had only minimal direct contact with her mother. There appeared to be no functional rules for contact except as exemplified in the brief play incident which occurred in the first session.

d. Parents talk about problems, children act them out. No one directly confronts each other.

e. Family members tend to compete or to pair-off to assure their position in the family. The flexibility of separateness and/or relating to different people at different times, as appropriate to need and pleasure, is not evidenced.

3. Rewards and Limitations of This System (see p. 20)

The price of maintaining the dysfunctional rules seems to be distance between family members, limitations on sexual development, unmet emotional needs and misspent energy. The payoffs may be low-risk, intellectual development at the price of intimacy and diversion from areas of distress. These payoffs previously had been functional but now with changing needs and changing family situation are dysfunctional.

4. <u>Individuals in the System</u> (As they influence the family functioning; see p. 15.)

Each member possesses strong, influencing characteristics. These characteristics are listed as follows:

a. Sara's self-image affects her ability to relate to Marie in this phase of Marie's development.

b. Harold's lack of comfort with his sexuality and with his normal sexual feelings toward his daughter affect his ability to relate to Marie in this stage of her development.

c. Marie seems recently to have experienced change in herself and consequently her internal rules are in flux, affecting her ability to relate to the entire family. She is striving for individual identity and her parents' difficulties are not helping her to take this step.

d. Jennifer and Tracy, particularly, seem to be lost in the competitive model of family interaction and have not established individual autonomy or feelings of self worth.

e. Anne is experiencing processes of separation from her mother, and broadening the scope of her world as she enters school, and is making internal adjustments accordingly. Where she fits into the system of the family now that she is not so attached to mother is a point of confusion to her.

5. <u>Context</u> (see p. 21)

Harold and Sara married with the anitcipation of children. Perhaps the foundations of intimacy in their relationship with each other were ill-formed at the time they began having children. The children, arriving in successive two-year intervals, forced family energies into parenting and the development of the marital relationship was some-what neglected. Both parents had an incomplete resolution of their adolescent conflicts, influencing the degree of ability they now possess with which to help their children in this Phase.

6. <u>Flexibility</u> (see p. 20)

Sara's ability to move away from Harold, in the first session, Marie's ability to come out of the corner, and Jennifer and Tracy's ability to achieve more separate

identities when all the children are not present in the
structured interview, are some indications of the family's
flexibility to change, giving the counselor indication of
a high degree of possibility for change. While some
resistance has been met in unveiling the system and, thus,
upsetting its balance, the strength of resistance does not
offset the range of flexibility.

7. Equilibrium (see pp. 20-21)

The dysfunctional facts of equilibrium in this family are
that equilibrium is gained in part by parents keeping
emotions under control and children expressing emotions in
activity--not always constructively. Sara, in the first
session with her tears, calls attention to this dysfunctional equilibrium. Equilibrium has been obtained at the
price of not developing individuality. Marie upset this
balance by her acting-out behavior.

8. Communication Patterns in the Family

In this family, problems are characteristically demonstrated by behavior rather than by being made known
explicitly by verbal means. To convert the meaning of
behavior first into awareness, and then into clear communication is the process necessary to allow meaningful contact, and thus allow constructive decision making to occur
among family members.

All these elements of the family system, seen in the light
of the presenting problem, illuminate Marie's behavior as
symptomatic of family dysfunctioning. Total family counseling
is the mode of further work selected. The counselor feels
each individual could benefit from focus on the aspects of
each of their lives affected by the system, and can be benefited by awareness of how their behavior affects the system.
The presence of all family members is a preventive measure
against Marie's problems recurring with the younger children.
Marie will gain reinforcement for change by the development of
a more nurturing system and her symptoms should dissipate as
the family system changes.

One should note that while these dysfunctional elements
are the focus of counseling, the counselor nonetheless sees
and supports the growth-enhancing elements of the system, such
as the family's strong motivation toward health, their active
attempts to reach each other, their base of caring and commitment to one another, and their high levels of functioning in
other areas of life, such as in intellectual and academic
pursuits.

With the foregoing assessment in mind and with recognition
that most of these factors have already been an explicit part
of the counseling process thus far experienced, the counselor
recognized the next session would likely be the transition
session to Phase II, a session of review and contract.

Session Three--Review and Contracting

The session began with reflections on the previous session
and the events of the past week. Jennifer complained that
promises had been broken during that time, and that her parents
had not spent time with her. Tracy chimed in with the same
complaint. The girls were encouraged to convey their feelings
about this directly to their parents and they expressed their
disappointment. In the ensuing discussion, the focus was on
the parents' difficulty and guilt feelings in saying "No,"
resulting either in frequently saying "Yes" when "No" was
meant, or in avoiding the questions and requests put to them.
Consequently, the children did not know when a "Yes" meant
"Yes." The girls reassured their parents that "No" was easier
to accept if it were clear, and if the parents said why the
answer was "No" and if there were sometimes also "Yeses."

The counselor then suggested that much had been learned
about the family in the past sessions and that this information
be reviewed so that determination could be made together of
what to do at this point in the counseling process. The counselor suggested that describing together their family's unique
way of interacting, how their way is helpful to them and also
how it hinders them, might aid all of them in understanding
the family better. Harold inquired as to how this could be
done and the counselor suggested that every family has "rules"
they tend to go by with each other. She suggested a few rules
she had noted in this family. She began with the rule,
"Parents try to figure out problems by talking, and children
tend to distract them or to show problems by action." Reference was made to the first session and some laughs were shared
about this rule. The counselor suggested areas in which rules
are made in families (see pp. 16-19). The counselor then
directed a discussion of families' rules and listed theirs on
large paper so all could see the list as these rules were
enumerated. Eventually the rules on p. 96 were mentioned by either family or counselor. The following were
added:

"Yeses" and "nos" are not clear.

Being special and different in this family is hard.

COUNSELING PRINCIPLE: In Phase I, in particular, the
counselor's role is sometimes that of a teacher. The

counselor has knowledge of ways a family can more clearly understand their interaction both by virtue of training and by the counselor's position as an outsider to the system. The counselor may directly impart knowledge as a teacher (See Table 2, Phase I p. 59). In Phase II, the counselor is less concerned with direct teaching and more concerned with being a guide toward experiential learning (See Phase II Table 3, p. 102).

Other characteristics of the family system were offered and then goals of counseling were discussed. Harold wanted to continue work on his and Marie's relationship, and Marie expressed the same desire. Each family member expressed concern about the father's relationships in the family, and it was generally agreed that this area would be explored further. Both the parents and children were interested in the specialness of each child and in the uniqueness of each. Marie was interested in having her family understand that she was different from them and that she wanted, therefore, to be treated differently. That the family had difficulty in showing warmth and affection and in asking for it directly was a pattern of behavior suggested by the counselor, and to change this pattern was a goal the group adopted. The indirect and competitive manner of letting needs be known also was discussed. To change this situation was another goal set for the counseling sessions.

The counselor stated that one of her goals, in addition to helping the family with their goals, was to work with Marie and her teacher to help apply in the classroom what was learned in the counseling sessions. The counselor sought and received agreement with Marie to meet with the counselor and the teacher as it seemed profitable to the progress of the counseling. All the family agreed that information from these sessions which could be helpful to Marie in the classroom could be shared confidentially, of course, with the teacher. If, at some later point, any family member felt they wanted certain information to be kept in confidence among this group, they would let their preferences be known. An agreement to meet was verified for a total of ten to twelve sessions.

With a system's assessment, a climate of trust and openness set and a contract established for goals and directions, the counseling moved into Phase II. (See Table 2, Phase I, p. 59, to check for completion of tasks.)

PHASE II - APEX OF COUNSELING - IN CASE EXAMPLE

In the second Phase of counseling the family moves
with more emotional impact into areas of conflict in which
they were wanting change. Experiencing the destructive elements and ways in which one's self may confront a problem to
change it, was the first focus of Phase II. The counselor
creates opportunities for the family to gain awareness of
factors that are inhibiting growth in their system and its
members.

The communication process is the counselor's main tool in
aiding change in Phase II. The task is to guide the family
toward change by facilitating constructive communication
between family members.

Intervention occurs at points where communication fails
to be effective. At these points the counselor introduces
methods that are felt to be appropriate to increase problem
awareness and to improve quality of communication.

Phase II is a continual cycle on a continuum of AWARENESS--
COMMUNICATION--OUTCOMES (or Decision). The family gains emotional awareness and an intellectual awareness of problem
areas in their interaction. They are assisted in communicating
with each other. On the basis of these two steps, new and
more satisfying outcomes or decisions can occur.

However small or large the decision the family has to make,
its quality is determined by the quality of awareness and
communication that precedes it. Effective counselors need not
suggest decisions or outcomes. The counselor facilitates increased quality of awareness and communication and the family
has tools to make more constructive decisions for their
approach.

As Phase II progresses, family members will begin to be
aware of their own destructive rules and patterns of behavior.
Consequently, they will begin to make their own intervention
and counselor intervention becomes less necessary. Some
emotional distance from the distress that has encompassed them
is gained and they begin to see humor in problems and to laugh
at them. Humor is an indication of integration of new learning.
The problem is less in the foreground. New awareness and
communication patterns gradually become more natural. The
system has begun to take on a new balance with more growth-
enhancing rules or patterns of behavior. These are indications
of progress toward the Closure Phase.

A Table of Phase II follows as does the continuation of
the Williams' case illustrating this Phase.

TABLE 3. PHASE II OF FAMILY COUNSELING (Apex Phase)

Counselor's Major Roles and Nature of Interaction	Tasks	Hoped-For Outcomes
Role: Guide toward change.	1. Continue and deepen Phase I tasks.	1. Continue Phase I outcomes.
Nature of Interaction	2. Increase individual and family awareness.	2. Increased awareness of problem areas in self and system.
1. Is less verbally active. People talk less with counselor, more with each other.	3. Feelings and behavior of family members change in areas of conflict as counselor.	3. Increased ability to risk change and experience success in making change.
2. Interventions are mostly for the purpose of facilitating family's interaction with each other.	a. created opportunities for corrective interactional experiences based on family's new awareness.	4. Increased ability to experience one's own power to make change and to try new behaviors.
	b. facilitates the efforts of the family as they try new behaviors.	5. Increased ability to see humor in problems and to laugh at self.
		6. Systems beginning to take on new equilibrium with more growth-enhancing rules and behavior patterns in operation.

102

Session Four--Family Sculpturing Technique

In this session Harold again raises the matter of his concern about Marie's getting the help she needs. In answer to
the counselor's request to him to review what is now understood
about Marie, the father speaks about her entering adolescence,
about her reaction toward having many sisters and wanting
attention for herself, and about her feelings relative to her
mother's being gone from the house more often. He cannot,
however, describe any of Marie's behavior with regard to himself, nor his and Marie's relationship. Marie's response to
her father is, "I am different from everyone else in the family." This statement is a familiar one from Marie, and the
counselor asks her to tell her father how she is different.
She seems unable to describe what she means, though her feelings seem strong. The counselor suggests that she use a
family sculpture to show how she sees her family and her relationship to it.

Family Sculpturing Technique. Sculpturing is done by
means of instructing one family member to move other family
members physically into a "sculpture" position, as seen by the
"sculptor." Family members then are placed into a configuration in relation to one another. This sculpture may involve
motionlessness on the part of the subjects, or they may be seen
in action. The subjects may be placed on the floor, on chairs,
or in any position which the sculptor feels is apt. The subjects are asked to move only as requested by the sculptor.

The counselor may instruct the sculptor to this effect:

I would like you to move each member of your family. Each
member will be like clay in your hands, and will move
where you want them to move. I would like you to try to
arrange them in any fashion--up, down, high, low, sitting,
moving, close to whomever you feel they are close to,
away from those from whom you think they are away--so
that the way you place them will show how you see the
family members in relation to each other.

The counselor assists the sculptor in considering details
of how each person should be placed. For example, the sculptor
might be reminded to situate the subject's head as the sculptor
sees it, or to instruct the subject to focus his eyes where
the sculptor believes them to be looking. The counselor is
careful to ask questions that can help the sculptor in arranging the sculpture to his own satisfaction without, however,
asking leading questions which might suggest a way of arranging
the family. The sculptor may keep moving both himself and
others until he feels that the sculpture correctly represents
the family as he sees it.

Finally, the sculptor is asked to place self in the sculpture where he/she envisions he/she is. In order to give the sculptor the "observing ego" view, a chair or some other object can be used to represent the individual in the sculpture while the sculptor moves out to check to see if the individual has created personal feelings about the family.

This activity contains many silences and time is taken to quietly experience the feeling of one's position in the sculpture or, if movement is required, one's pattern. The sculptor then is asked to express feelings about the sculpture that has been created, and each family member may be asked to describe their feeling about the position in which they have been placed.

The counselor keeps the control of this sculpture in the hands of the sculptor. Other family members may want to change configuration, but focus is maintained on this sculptor's impressions for the time being, in order to allow a deeper effect to develop. Family members may be reminded by the counselor that they will have their opportunity to create a sculpture, and that the aim at present is to respond to the sculptor's requests.

After the sculptor has explained feelings about the sculpture, a re-arrangement may be made, (with the benefit of the feelings that have just been experienced and the comments that have just been received from the other family members) into a manner that represents how the sculptor wishes the family configuration might be. Family members then may react to the new arrangement, and participate in a discussion as to what might occur in the family to permit the desired changes that have been indicated. Other family members then may do their version of the sculpture.

Family sculpturing generally is highly charged with emotion. Members are experiencing feelings, not merely talking about them. The nonverbal facet of this activity often touches many areas that previously have been only partially encountered (and, perhaps, frequently avoided) by family members. Consequently, the activity serves not only to unveil the system to those within it, but also to encourage the experience of feelings about the system which is necessary for change. Expression of these activated feelings can be focused by the counselor so that communication follows the frequently deep feelings brought on by the sculpture.

As an example of facilitating these hitherto unrealized feelings, the following exchange might take place:

FAMILY MEMBER: (With pain in his voice) I don't like
mother sitting on the floor.

COUNSELOR: How do you feel when she is sitting on the
floor?

FAMILY MEMBER: I feel I can't get to her.

COUNSELOR: You feel you can't get to her and you
would like to?

FAMILY MEMBER: Yes.

COUNSELOR: Say this to her.

The dialogue which follows may break past barriers in communication which have long been present.

Sculpturing can be used in other forms, such as drawing
a sculpture (or a family sociogram) if families are hesitant
to act it out. The group as a whole may draw one sociogram,
or each individual may draw a sociogram and discuss it with
the family. As the family members are talking, the counselor
may suggest physical postures that would bodily express what
they are saying, thus, assisting them in creating a sculpture.

Sculpturing is an imaginative exercise for both counselor
and family and an effective means to break beyond the limits
of words. This technique permits visualizing and experiencing
system facets that further unveil the system and help make
explicit what is implied. The activity gives focus to discrepancy between what is talked about and what is done, and
between the reality and the wish. Goals and routes for change
can evolve from such an activity, and/or the limiting realities
can be faced and disappointments dealt with if mutual desire
for change does not exist.

Limitations come from this technique as with most techniques. If the technique form should be held to the point of
ignoring the process occurring among members, that is if the
technique is allowed to become an end in itself rather than
a means toward creating interaction; or if the interpretation
of the sculpture is rigidly observed rather than used merely
as a bridge between words and feelings, the value of the
technique is lost. Used properly, however, and at those times
when it seems most appropriate, this technique is one of the
most helpful tools in the family counseling process.

The Sculpture Technique and the Williams Family. Marie
created a sculpture of her family in which all the family
members were in a line. First Jennifer, then Tracy, Anne, Sara

105

Marie's Family Sculpture
"Marie created a sculpture of her family
in which all of the family members werer
in a line."

and Harold. Marie placed a chair at the end of the line, by
Jennifer, stood on the chair, leaped past all her family,
touched her father, and fell onto the mats she had piled at
the other end of the line past her father.

She was not able to put the meaning of the action into
words. It wasn't in her conscious awareness. The counselor
kept describing what Marie was doing as Marie repeated the
leaping action two or three times. "You leap past all your
family, touch your father, and fall on the mats." Marie confirmed the description and added, "I brace myself for the big
jump and then crash."

The counselor remarked, "You have to get past a lot of
folks to get to your dad; then you don't quite do it."

Marie blushed.

Harold's awareness of how he previously felt close to
Marie and no longer did was evoked.

When the question of resculpturing was posed, Marie
declared that she didn't want to "play the game anymore." When
asked if she would if her father continued and if he directed
it, she agreed. Harold was invited to recreate the sculpture
to show either how his and Marie's relationship used to be, or
how he would like it to be now. Tension, a creative tension,
was high with all the family members. Harold tried to catch
Marie's eye, but when she would not look at him, he said he
would not do either of those suggested sculptures then but
would wait until another time. The counselor expressed again
her observation of the caring of the family members, the wish
for closeness and yet the caution. Feeling that Harold and
Marie needed some interval before pursuing their relationship
further, she expressed this and then elicited Sara's response
to the session, and then Jennifer's, Tracy's, and Anne's. They
saw the depth of feeling and emotionally related to it.
"Everybody fights for people to listen to them," Tracy
announced. The session ended with an acute awareness of this
problem area. An area of commonality of feeling had been
experienced, and warmth was present between members. As the
session ended, the family had a focus for their work for the
following week, it seemed, and they now seemed more deeply
committed to the process of counseling and the process of
change.

Session Five--Direct Communication by Complete-a-Sentence Technique

Session Five began with Tracy and Anne fighting over who
would have the chair beside Sara. All of the members at the

session watched the fight. Tracy got her way by pulling Anne
out of the chair and Anne then sat on the floor and cried.
Sara pulled Anne toward her and put her on her lap. The focus
of the Session became the problem of four children, close in
age, competing for attention. The common difficulty of all
family members in asking for what they want and in giving
clear answers, the counselor pointed out, was a contributing
factor in this problem. Tracy was asked how she knew when she
was loved by others in the family, and what she knew about
how to ask for what she wanted without fighting. Her responses
were very unclear. She was asked to stand in front of each
person in the family, one at a time, and announce, "I would
like to be special to you. I would like for us (or you) to
_____(completing the sentence as she wished)."
Here is an example of what occurred.

TRACY: (To Mother) I would like to be special to
you, Mom. (Laughed a little, uncomfort-
ably) I would like for you to play with me
more.

SARA: Sometimes I am too busy.

The counselor asked Sara to first give her feeling response
to Tracy before explaining why she did not play with her.

SARA: I like how you are right now, Tracy. I
liked your giggle and the way you touched
my hand as you talked. (She stopped and
the counselor asked her to go on with her
feeling response about the request) I
would like to play with you more. Sometimes I feel bad because I can't because
I am too busy.

COUNSELING PRINCIPLE: The task of the counselor
is to facilitate communication by inviting expression
of feeling, as well as by being sure that what is
heard is what is said and what is said is what is felt.
Awareness of feeling and clarity in communication
must be achieved before the family is ready to move
toward decision making and alternative behaviors.

The difference in Tracy's feeling toward this fuller
response was obvious. The issue then was addressed as to how
Tracy and Sara could handle the situation of Tracy's having a
wish and Sara's sharing that wish when the timing for ful-
filling the wish was inappropriate to Mother's schedule. This
situation referred us back to the need for the parents to say
"No" when "No" was felt and hopefully, of offering when "Yes"
would be possible. Tracy reassured her mother that "No" was

108

okay if sometimes Sara would play with her. The fear of being overwhelmed by requests from the family seemed to diminish somewhat more in Sara. With some laughter there was discussion that it would even be okay for Sara to say "No" if she had a preference for something else she wanted to do, for herself or with Harold, or with another person, at that moment. In other words "No" did not have to signify that she was too busy. Sara and Harold both, laughingly recognized this problem in themselves. There was some teasing from the counselor about their having the "people helper's disease."

> COUNSELING PRINCIPLE: As Phase II progresses, family members become increasingly less guilty or blameful of self and others when problems are revealed. They are able to see humor in their behaviors and laugh at themselves. Humor is a facilitator to change and an indication of progress. (See TABLE 2, PHASE I, Hoped-For Outcomes," p. 59.)

As the session progressed, this technique of Completing a Sentence continued to focus on each member's ability to confront another family member with what they wanted in their relationship with them. The technique is a simple way of lending focus to an area of specific concern in a family. By addressing one person at a time, using the individual's name, standing in front of that person and stating, "I want," direct contact obviously is facilitated, as much by the content discussed as by the process by which it is said.

As you will notice, more planned exercises are introduced into the last two sessions. This is done to more quickly unveil the family system and move more readily to the points of focus for change. These same elements would likely be revealed in time in counseling without the techniques, but with the time limit, they are particularly useful, and this family is responsive to them.

Session Six--Drama, Doubling, and Empty-Chair Techniques

Once again Harold brought up the matter of how he used to be closer to Marie and yet, when he had come home late during the past week, and had known she was upset, he didn't go to her or try to help her with whatever was bothering her. He said he was upset with himself for this, and he apologized to Marie. He further reported that one night he had tried to help Marie with her homework, but that she had gotten angry at him and he gave up the attempt. As her father talked,

109

Marie seemed to be withdrawing, as she had in the corner at the First Session. To facilitate a breakthrough of this impass, a drama situation was created.

Drama Technique. Drama in counseling is a psychodramatic technique which is used to re-create a situation of conflict for the purpose of bringing painful experiences of the past into the present situation. This, in turn, brings the painful effect into the present moment and once the real emotion is present in the context of this created situation, not only can the problem and its dimensions be more clearly seen than when talking about them, but opportunity can be created for gaining understanding of the problem and trying new behaviors.

The Doubling Technique. When, in the process of re-enacted dialogue, the counselor sees an incongruency between what the person is saying and the person's behavior, or hears a double message in the spoken words, the counselor can become that person's "double" and by speaking as if the counselor were that person, may bring out the incongruency and so facilitate a clearer and more direct message to the receiver. Being a double is a way of providing input into the drama situation without interrupting the drama itself. It may facilitate the speaker in being more aware of internal dialogue and in communicating it more clearly. An example follows later in this session with the Williams.

Empty-Chair Technique. Sometimes a sideline talk with a double is not enough to work out one's internal dialogue problems so that one is able to send a clearer message. Sometimes too many voices within oneself are speaking, and it is necessary to have time to talk to these internal parts if a congruent message is to be sent. If at such times the counselor is thinking in images, visualizing the person's internal parts in terms of opposite pulls, the counselor can set up two chairs to illustrate the opposite pulls within the person and then have that person perform a dialogue with these symbolized opposites as a means of reaching sufficient synthesis within one's self to be able to communicate more clearly. This technique, too, is illustrated within the following dramatic presentation.

Drama Technique With Harold And Marie. The situation when Harold attempted to help Marie with her homework was re-created. The stage was set by talking about what her room looked like, and then by simulating it in the meeting room. Marie had been on her bed when Harold came in, so mats were placed on the floor and Marie laid on them "doing her homework." Harold came in. He spoke to her and asked if he could help her. Marie responded, "Aw, I guess so," which was an answer ambivalent enough to leave Harold in doubt of what she

wanted. He remained standing at the door looking puzzled.
The first impass had occurred.

At this point, the counselor suggested that she would pretend to be Harold's double and say certain things to him. If
he disagreed, he could ignore what she had said; if he agreed
he could do or say what the counselor had suggested but in
his own way. The persons present would pretend that no one
but Harold could hear what the counselor said to him.

COUNSELOR-HAROLD: How do I feel just now?

HAROLD: Oh, I want to help.

COUNSELOR-HAROLD: But I'm not so sure about how it will
                   work out. (Harold nods and the coun-
                   selor continues) I used to be able to
                   help my daughter without all this con-
                   flict. What is happening now?

HAROLD: (TO   I don't know; something is, but I do
COUNSELOR DOUBLE) want to help.

COUNSELOR-HAROLD: I think I'll go in!

HAROLD: No, she hasn't asked me.

COUNSELOR-HAROLD: Then I think I will leave.

HAROLD: No, I want to help.

On hearing Harold say that he wanted to help and yet observing
him seemingly frozen at the door, the counselor was aware of
two sides of Harold's inner conflict. A chair was placed just
inside the door and one just outside it, and the counselor
explained to Harold that one chair represented the side of him
that said, "I want to go in and help," and the other, the side
that said, "I don't know about this. . .it is not like it
used to be."

Harold moved from chair to chair, carrying on a debate
between the two sides of himself, and as he did so, he began
to clarify the opposing sides as follows: "I want to be close
to my daughter. . .but. . .I had better be careful how close I
get to her now. . .she is getting to be such an attractive
lady and fathers had better keep their distance."

The two chairs were set up for Marie in order to assist
her in looking at her ambivalent response. She labeled one as,
"Sure, I want him to help me," and the other as, "Oh, I don't
like me and probably he doesn't either." In the process of

111

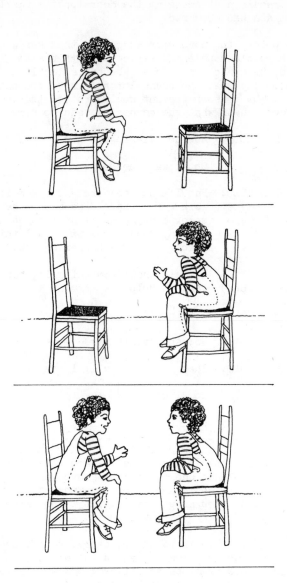

She labeled one as, "Sure, I want him
to help me," and the other as, "Oh, I
don't like me and probably he doesn't
either."

sitting first in one chair and then the other, trying to convince the opposite side of the justification of her position, the side that stated the wish for help was re-defined into the side of Marie that liked herself and felt she was lovable and that it was okay to be lovable; while the other side began to argue that she was neither pretty nor deserving of love. These redefinitions were suggested by the counselor after hearing Marie say the same things in a less acute way.

Marie became tearful and silence prevailed while everyone shared her pain. The counselor shared with Marie the fact that she had felt that way too about herself, and that she hurt too when she doubted her lovability. Sara shared the same information. That Harold seemed not to feel so good about himself at the door to her room also was mentioned, and Harold agreed. All of the family seemed to make a deep feeling contact. Anne moved toward Marie, and Jennifer threw a tissue in Marie's direction. There seemed to be an acute awareness, each person of their own feelings and of their common humanity.

This moment might be described as a family peak experience (see p. 7.) The family system changes are illustrated here. Feelings are openly recognized and empathy is expressed instead of ignoring feeling or competing for the group's attention as was present earlier in Phase I. The family system has begun to take on a new balance. (See TABLE 3, PHASE II "Hoped-For Outcomes," p. 102.)

To strengthen the part of Marie that felt good about herself, the counselor asked Marie to face the chair that represented that part of herself. The counselor stood beside Marie, put her arm around Marie, and asked Marie, "Tell me about that Marie what do you like about her?" First with coaxing and then more easily, Marie talked about the things she liked about herself, and each comment she made was met with support by the different family members and the counselor. They added additional things about Marie which they liked and that she had not mentioned. Then Marie sat in the chair of the "Marie" about whom she had been talking, and was asked to look as if she knew all those things to be true. When she had trouble doing this, Tracy demonstrated the knack for Marie by sitting tall and looking proud. This action brought giggles from everyone, a sort of laughter-relief to the situation. But it was a supportive laugh, and seemed to bring the drama to some closure. The counselor then asked Harold if he would ask Marie if he could help her, or perhaps just offer her some caring without asking. Harold moved closer to Marie and touched her shoulder; Marie looked up and giggled. A period of silence occurred in which the pleasure of the contact seemed to be felt and then the drama was ended by the four girls exiting to the yard to play.

Sara walked behind them. Harold lingered, seemingly for reassurance. The good feeling of moving closer was reinforced by a remark from the counselor, who also suggested that the ability to move apart, when that feels right, also had just happened. This moving apart was different than before--it was not fearful or defensive but more like a celebration. Harold's comments indicated pleasure with himself and an understanding of the counselor comments.

The drama technique of working in this case was simply a brief catalyst to move Marie and Harold into their feelings and then move them on past the feelings which were stopping them from having contact with each other. Within the context of the drama, whatever dramatic techniques that suggest themself to the visually-thinking counselor could be employed to make the dialogue more graphic. For example, if one member seemed to be talking to another, but not to be emotionally present while speaking, the counselor might have that person turn away and continue the conversation. If the conversation were between a person communicating as an authority figure and a second person communicating as a helpless victim or placator to that person, member one standing in the chair and the other member standing on knees might dramatically illustrate the conversation. Drama is helpful in recall of feeling; it is helpful in more acutely experiencing an area of conflict and in recreating situations where alternatives then can be acted out. Unlike a play in which acting is the aim, here the learning experience is facilitated.

Second Teacher-Counselor Conference

Periodically during the time of family counseling, the counselor and Marie's teacher have talked. The counselor has offered support in the teacher's endeavors with Marie, and has shared information from the counseling sessions that seemed pertinent or parallel to the classroom situation. After the sixth counseling session, the teacher has reported incidents of Marie's explosions with classmates followed by withdrawal. While the teacher's relationship with Marie has improved, the conflict between Marie and other students has not. Marie's teacher is baffled by this behavior.

Marie and her teacher met for a role-playing session of one of these incidents. In the session, an incident is recalled and replayed in a drama and the counselor directs the drama as she does with the family (see p. 110). As the conflict of the situation approaches, Marie is asked to turn her head to the side (no longer talking with the student--played by the teacher--with whom she is having the conflicts), and to say what she is feeling. It becomes apparent that here, as in the family situation, Marie's feelings of low esteem for herself are contributing to the creation of situations where she is rejected by other students. (This pattern is as it happened in the drama with her father.) She deals with these school situations as she copes with similar situations at home; she has what is labeled as a temper tantrum or burst of anger and then withdraws. It is after such incidents that she has stolen pencils and small school items from the student whom she felt was rejecting her.

In this session, Marie became aware of how she contributed to this problem, both at home and at school. What Marie can do at these times is the question, as well as what kind of action from the teacher might be helpful to Marie in dealing with her feelings. Building her strengths, as one way of increasing self-esteem, was suggested, and the teacher and Marie talked about what Marie did or could do in school that might help her to feel better about herself; and what she did or could do to help herself develop a feeling of being liked by other students. A few specific and simple experiences, which seemed most likely to provide success endeavors, were decided.

The family counseling seemed to have assisted Marie in more readily recognizing her role in classroom conflict, and in providing the supportive climate necessary for her to be able to assume responsibility for her behavior, and to work toward change. This supportive climate further strengthened the relationship between Marie and her teacher. Realizing the parallels in her home and her classroom behavior now provided for Marie two environments supportive to Marie's instigation of change. The risk of self exposure that Marie was able to take in this session likely could not have been done without the successful completion of Phase I and many of the tasks and anticipated outcomes of Phase II (see Tables--Phase I, p. 59, and Phase II, p. 102). Timing, then, is a most critical issue in constructively asking for the risk of self exposure.

Session Seven--Parts Technique

The counselor opened this Session with a discussion about Session Six. There had been little time for closure of the last session and the counselor felt a sense of the session having been unfinished. She recalled how Marie had stated she felt herself lovable but sometimes doubted it. Sara related her feelings that were similar to Marie's. Sara had concern about her attractiveness to her husband, especially as she was getting older. Marie began to look concerned. The counselor felt that Marie needed assurance and did assure Marie that she had not caused this problem. Marie took the reassurance and seemed relieved. The counselor invited Marie and Sara to share their similar feelings. They shared about themselves as females with more comfort than was seen previously. Some surprise and relief occurred as they experienced themselves not necessarily as mother and daughter, but as two human beings with similar feelings.

Sara was encouraged to talk to Harold about her concern. As the conversation evolved, it became clear that Harold and Sara related to each other most strongly with their efficiency-parts; that is, the parts of themselves that organized their household, tended to eating, cooking and managing a family; and that they related as a couple with friends but seldom as two individuals. They supported each other in their intellectual pursuits. However, Sara, in particular, felt she wanted other ways of relating, and especially a greater show of affection between she and her husband. Sara seemed to blame Harold for the problem and he defended himself. To break this circle, the counselor expressed her own feeling of frustration at the attack-blame game, and suggested that they add more dimension to the picture. She introduced the following technique.

The Parts Technique. The counselor asked Sara to identify what part of her did not feel attractive as a woman. She was asked to sculpt the part of her by using one of the children, giving the child a body position that would illustrate the part of her that felt unattractive. Tracy volunteered.

When asked to visualize and define other parts of herself, Sara described a very competent, professional part and a part she called "household efficiency." As further discussion continued with the counselor and family, a part for a helpless little girl was added to the collection. (The counselor assured Sara that most of us have this part somewhere in us.) And finally, a part for a sexual woman was added. Sara represented each of these parts with an object or a person. Marie was chosen to be her "sexy" part. Marie assumed the position with a wiggle of her buttocks and a laugh.

Harold was asked if he were aware of parts of himself. Harold mentioned a few and, when coaxed by the family, mentioned more. Jennifer played Harold's gruff part, holding people at a distance. Harold's indifference was symbolized by a book he might read to avoid people. His "sexy" part was found in a magazine by Tracy and Jennifer, a handsome man in a suit and tie. It became a game to choose appropriate objects to represent parts.

With some of Harold's and Sara's parts thus visualized, the counselor asked them to greet one another at the door. Sara was asked to decide which of her parts would be in the foreground as she greeted Harold. Harold put his intellectual-

The Inner Voice May Be Very Different
From the Outer Mask We Wear

The counselor listens for feelings when
words, voice, tone, eyes and body posture
are not congruent with each other.

philosopher part in the foregound. Sara tried several different combinations. When Harold's intellectual-philosopher self was in his foreground, and Sara's loving sensual self was in her foreground, they clashed at the greeting.

When Sara's affectionate part was in the foreground Harold was unable to recognize it at once. (A repeated theme was seen: in this family, when warm feelings were either felt or wanted, frequent miscommunication resulted.) Harold was given an opportunity to respond differently in a fresh trial. The scene was set. Sara met him at the door feeling affectionate and sensual. (Some work was done with Sara to help her to give a strong, congruent message.) Harold tried several responses: he teased her, he told her to "go away for now," he gave her a hug.

Several different combinations of parts were tried with different scenes and some situations from the past were re-enacted with the opportunity to try different behaviors. Sara and Harold were laughing at themselves and each other and the children joined in. It was funny to see Sara try to reach Harold by indirect messages which requested affection, such as by saying that she had made him a good dinner, and to watch him miss the message totally with his nose in the book, saying "In a moment, dear," thinking that her message was merely a call to dinner; and all the while Marie danced around behind her mother like the sensual part of Sara that was hiding behind her efficiency. Marie's delight at this role was recognized and pointed out to Sara in particular. Sara and Marie reversed roles to give Sara an opportunity to experience this part of herself and as she did emotional recognition of the problem being confronted seemed to have come full circle, so to speak. That is, it seemed Sara recognized her hesitancy to ask for affection or show it, and she saw the basis of this being her doubts about her lovability. Before she had thought the problem to be her husband's. Now she would assume responsibility for her part in it. (See TABLE 3, PHASE II, Hoped-For Outcomes p. 102.)

Marie identified a similar issue in herself as did Harold. Jennifer, Tracy and Ann related to the subject as well. Role playing was done, trying out different behaviors such as asking directly for needs to be met. The Session ended with goals in mind for practicing these new behaviors during the following week.

The parts technique is illustrated in Figure 2 as shown on p. 119.

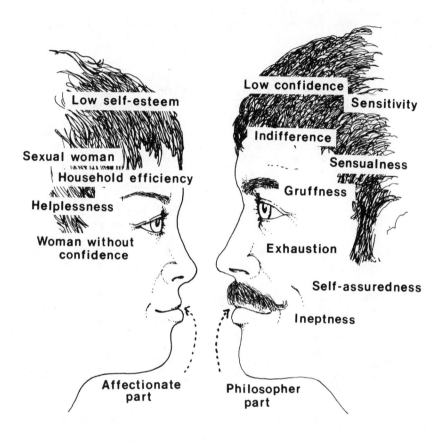

Figure 2. Foreground/Background of Some
of Sara's and Harold's Parts

The closer to the back of the figure, the more in the
background is that part, and conversely the nearer
the front of the head the part represents foreground
feelings at a particular moment.

119

When Sara greets Harold on his arrival home with her "affectionate" part and he responds with his "philosopher" part, they do not make contact. This lack of contact is not because one or the other is bad or wrong but simply reflects their psychological space at that moment. Taking this incident as a comment about self or other worth would be dysfunctional behavior. It would result in self or other blame. If such behavior is reacted to in a growth framework several choices of response are possible. Some examples are the following:

1. Harold and Sara may remain with their same parts in the foreground and remain in or out of each other's presence, but accept each other's position and not demand different behavior from each other.

2. They may either or both rearrange their internal parts so that the part in the foreground for each of them complements the other, yet does not invade the other's integrity, so that they will make contact.

3. They may directly request for needs to be met by the other, accepting the response as a comment about the other's state of being and choice for the moment, and not as a comment about self worth. Disappointment can be accepted when in a growth framework.

4. They may go away from each other for the moment and meet their needs in other ways themselves, or turn to someone else and then come back together when their parts are more complementary.

The diagram may be used with the parts technique in counseling, particularly with families who may be more hesitant to express themselves in action.

Sessions Eight and Nine--Variation of the Parts Technique

The parts idea seemed to kindle such enthusiasm with the children and Harold and Sara, that they all wished to continue with it. The idea seemed to lend itself to helping each individual identify and appreciate uniqueness of self, as well as to help the family see the uniqueness of its members. Since uniqueness was one of the areas of focus in the counseling process with the Williams, the technique was continued in the next sessions.

Variations on the Parts Technique. During Sessions Eight and Nine, each family member had a large sheet of butcher paper on which to draw symbolic features of themselves. Animals and objects could represent the parts; colors and shapes also were used. They also could make masks to wear

"One of Marie's Representative Parts Drawings"

which would represent their different faces. The family worked around a table.

After each member had worked out his own self perceptions, these were presented one by one to the rest of the family, and the uniqueness of the person being represented was discussed. Additional parts were suggested by other family members and, if accepted, were added. The interrelationship of the parts to each other (which ones came into the foreground and when) was discussed, and the family recalled incidents which illustrated their assertions. Parts which the person wanted to nurture in him/her self were discussed and requests were made as to how family members might help with this change. Specific times when one is disappointed in self were mentioned, and discussion was held on what can be done to help oneself with disliked parts and how family can help.

As an example of this version of the parts technique, Marie's interaction with the family was discussed. Marie saw herself as being more shy than she previously had been, and also quieter and more in need of privacy than any other member of the family. To her, the other family members seemed highly interactive. Marie saw herself as almost the opposite of her mother on the "outside," but added that on the "inside" they felt a lot alike. Sara had worried when Marie was not interactive, and pushed Marie to be more interactive within the family unit. With Marie's new ability to communicate her need for separateness and solitude, Sara now understood this as a part of Marie's way of being, rather than as always a problem.

When her mother expressed the need for separateness as a problem, Marie replied, "Oh Mom, don't you know the difference between alone and lonely." Sara recalled that it was her own fear of loneliness that sometimes blocked her from the pleasures of being alone. In understanding more Marie's feelings, Sara could accept them and Sara experienced relief. Marie was reassured that the changes she had recently experienced in herself were all right; she did not have to be the way she used to be. However, Marie's family might expect her to be as she used to be unless she told them how she was now feeling. Telling her needs and asking for these needs would work far better than acting them out.

Marie spoke of a part of her that was lonely and wished for a good friend outside the family, and the family discussed how they might help her achieve that goal. It was pointed out that the family's willingness to help Marie did not enable them to know what she wanted unless she told them. Marie was somewhat surprised by the family's eagerness to help her and by their acceptance of her.

Tracy emerged as being rather shy herself, and expressed feelings of being bossed by Jennifer. It seemed that Tracy no longer needed the tight ties to Jennifer she once had, and could announce her wish for a change in the relationship. At different times Tracy identified with Marie, then with Anne, or with her father or her mother. A sense of fluidity with regard to separateness and closeness--the ability to move in and out with various family members--emerged as a desire in other family members as well.

This activity obviously merely utilized visual means of unveiling individual systems. Self-discovery and self-other-discovery were the significant foci of the exercise. These discoveries need to be absorbed slowly and with as much full-ness and feeling as possible, thus, the activity has many silences. Symbols are the language and are experienced as fully as possible without converting these symbols to narrowly defined verbalizations. Developing feeling of appreciation for self and other, and creating an enhanced ability to see more dimensions to self and other are counseling goals, and as these goals are achieved, individuals have more choices of behaviors and family members' interactions have more depth and creative possibilities.

One's own discovery of self is a first step in the activity, and sharing of self with family is secondary, supporting the earlier stated purpose of the family: "to create a vessel for the development of the mature, fully-functioning individual."

Counselor's Review of the Williams Family

Phase II seems to be moving toward a natural closure. More satisfying contact is being made between all family members in the process of the session; there are more direct requests for what one wants and there is more comfort in give-and-take in the family. More self-other respect is being shown in relationships, and competition has become less necessary in attempting to insure one's position in the family. Generally, more congruency exists among the family members between what a member feels and thinks and what is communicated. This relationship in turn allows more freedom for being one's individual and unique self. All of these factors have interrupted the operation of dysfunctional rules and have increased self-other awareness, the quality of communication, and the subsequent interactional outcomes. Marie's symptoms have dissipated and no new symptomology is evident in the family. The family is operating in a growth framework to a much larger extent than in the beginning of counseling, and growth-enhancing rules are in operation. (See pp. 15-19.)

Further work could be done with Harold and Sara toward enrichment of their relationship; however, to some degree they seem to have their own ideas on how to proceed in that direction, and sufficient freedom to do so. However, letting them know that couple referral is possible, may be indicated. This area of counseling is less in the confines of the original structure of the twelve sessions with this family.

Reviewing Phase II Table (p. 102) the task of this Phase has been completed. Though, of course all the goals of the family could be explored in much more depth, due to limited time of counseling, the counselor is now aware of the need to direct sessions toward the Closure Phase.

Third Teacher-Counselor Conference

Periodic and informal teacher-counselor contacts are made during Phase II to check the effects of family counseling on Marie's classroom behavior. The temper tantrums had ceased. Conversations between the teacher and Marie, and the change in Marie's relationship with classmates seemed to provide the teacher with positive affirmation of her work with Marie and with support to continue it. Marie seemed less distracted in the classroom, and as her concentration became better, her work had improved, though she was not the "top student" she once had been. She seemed to have less energy to focus on this matter. This fact was accepted by the teacher as she continued to help Marie with her self-image and her relationships with other students, both of which were Marie's more immediate needs.

Marie was more spontaneous in the classroom, no longer withdrawn. She seemed to be more comfortable with herself and with others. The counselor mentioned to Marie's teacher the work Marie had done in mask and poster representation of her parts. Because it seemed Marie was rather pleased with her work and might enjoy sharing it with her teacher, the two decided to ask her if she would. Marie was delighted with the request, and brought "herself" on paper to share with the teacher. The counselor joined Marie and the teacher one day after school in the classroom to share these creative endeavors. Applications from Marie's learning to classroom incidents that were evident to any of the three persons present were mentioned. The presentation seemed to be a summary of Marie's progressive change of behavior in the classroom and afforded a vehicle for teacher and student to communicate more clearly about a process they had been sharing. A team of three people working together toward problem resolution was what evolved in this session and each of the three persons involved shared this feeling.

PHASE III - CLOSURE PHASE - IN CASE EXAMPLE

In the Closure Phase of counseling, learning is integrated with behaviors. The family and the counselor review the course of counseling, goals, progress toward goals, new learnings, and changes; and the counselor supports what has been done. What "might have been done," is not relevant at this point, nor is new material explored.

Individual or couple referral, if desired and/or indicated, is discussed. Indications for further family counseling are discussed and the possibility of return for what might be called a "well family check up," (particularly at points of normal family life crises) is encouraged if the counselor's time schedule can at all provide such a preventive service.

Above all, however, the family's own new tools for change and for maintaining family health are reinforced. Areas of potential problems are reviewed, areas in which the family will need to pay close attention to their behaviors and use their new tools to break old patterns are brought to mind for secure placement in the thought patterns of each family member.

In the Closure Phase of counseling, separation between the family and the counselor is occurring. Feelings of appreciation, affection, disappointments and feelings of loss will need to be expressed by both counselor and family. Irritations and angers not handled at the time they occurred also may need to be expressed to finish any unfinished business and thus allow for termination. This time is one when the family is claiming their learnings and tools, and asserting on their own the positive abilities they have developed.

In the Closure Phase particularly, the counselor may learn from the family. The family can give the counselor feedback as to what the experience of counseling has been for them, so that the counselor has a chance to learn about some facets of personal effectiveness as a counselor which are impossible to learn except by listening to those whose lives have been affected.

A Table of Phase III follows as does case material illustrating the ending of counseling.

TABLE 4. PHASE III OF FAMILY COUNSELING (Closure Phase)--

Integration of Learning

Counselor's Major Role and Nature of Interaction	Tasks	Hoped-For Outcomes
Role	Continued practice of change	1. Continuation of Phase II outcomes.
1. Guide toward change – particularly integration of change.	1. Family continues practice of new behaviors and counselor gives support as needed, but gradually lessens this activity as need lessens; facilitates family members doing this for selves and each other.	2. Family members have more tools to help each other and themselves break old patterns that caused pain; and enhance strengths in themselves and the family.
Nature of interactions	Review and Integration of Learning	3. Family members have increased awareness of themselves individually and the family system.
1. Needs to make even fewer interventions as family interacts in more growth-enhancing ways.	2. Facilitates review, integration and closure of counseling.	4. Family members feel their own power to make constructive changes and the use of their power occurs in and out of sessions.
2. Less active: activity is more to facilitate family doing their own work.	Separation between family and counselor	5. A new balance is achieved that offers more flexibility and growth.
	3. Facilitates expression of feeling between family and counselor.	6. The above-mentioned outcomes tend to make the counselor's presence irrelevant.

Session Ten--Beginning of Review and Integration

The day of this session was sunny and warm, the first of spring-like days. When the Williams' arrived, Anne asked what we were going to do today, and then announced that she would like to play outside. The counselor asked her to remain inside until it had been decided what the group would do and Anne agreed.

Sara reported with pleasure that the semester break had come for her and that she and Harold were going to take a week-end trip. Marie seems to be happier at home, Sara reported, though less is seen of her because she reads in her room and goes to friends' houses after school. Sara misses her, but "it is okay." Marie interrupted, a bit agitated, "Mother, now you know I like to read."

The counselor said she had noticed many changes in the family and suggested that the session might be spent as a review day, to talk about what had changed, and to see if the family had made (or felt they were making) the changes they wanted to make during counseling. The counselor commented on the interaction that had just occurred between Sara and Marie as an example of change.

While Marie seemed to be holding strongly to her rights, perhaps somewhat in reaction against her mother, still the two people expressed their wishes and could allow the other to reach their own expression of themselves. Some respect for each other and some understanding seem to be in each of their attitudes. Anne was asked to join this discussion for awhile before she went out. Anne was asked what she liked about the family now, and about herself being a part of that family.

At first the review was absent of feeling, particularly with the children. The children seemed to be trying to respond to what was asked of them, so they could go out. A time limit of twenty minutes' conversation was set and seemed to give sufficient reassurance to them that there would be ample time in which to play, so that the children began to join in more freely. When the counselor recalled the first session and its fighting and irritation, and later the game of leap frog and the fun that was experienced, the children began to chime in with memories of making their masks, and of humorous incidents that had occurred in the sessions. Stories about what had happened at home were recounted.

As the conversation continued, whatever happened in its process that reflected the positive change in the family was noted and supported by the counselor. Family members, too, began to note their changes. There was, for example, more

interchange as people talked, and less competition. Everyone
seemed to feel their idea was important enough and they were
important enough to speak again if they hadn't been heard
the first time, and if they really wanted to be heard. Family
members seemed to share each other's joy.

Definite opinions, "yeses and nos," as they were felt were
spoken, but as a way of reporting clearly and directly what
family members thought or felt, not as a way to prove their
own worth or attack another. Different ideas and perceptions
could stand in the presence of each other. There was more
touching when people felt like touching each other, and more
eye contact. "How are you doing with the process of asking for
what you want and then discussing with each other a decision
about that want?" the counselor inquired. Some positive and
some negative experiences were reported, but generally what
individuals contributed to the negative experience was readily
available to their awareness, as well as how they might make
the situation different. For the most part, personal responsibility was being accepted.

The conversation seemed to reach some closure and Anne went
to the door and announced (while in effect asking) that she was
going outside. There was general positive response to her move
and, as she exited, she asked Tracy to join her. One by one,
all the children went out to play.

Watching the children through the glass door this time was
quite a different experience than watching their play early
in the sessions, the counselor remarked, and Harold and Sara
also seemed to be thinking of the contrast. Sara announced,
with self-pleasure, that she had gone on a diet. The counselor
supported her pleasure and asked about changes in the relationship between Harold and Sara. They both reported a more pleasurable sexual relationship and said they were giving themselves more time alone and more permission to enjoy themselves
and each other, not just sexually, but in other ways as well.

"Things aren't changed yet as much as we want them to
change, though," Harold and Sara agreed. There was discussion
of what they still wanted different and what they knew about
how to make it different, followed by a discussion of the
specific things they were going to do or could do to facilitate
change. Generally, both Sara and Harold seemed to understand
the problem areas. They had a mutual vocabulary and openness
now for talking about them, as well as some tools for making
change. The counselor suggested that they pay close attention
to even the slightest encounters containing these problems,
and that they slowly take the time and patience to work on
them. The counselor also cautioned them to take care not to

reprimand themselves or each other when things didn't go well, but to seek understanding so they would have more tools for change next time.

The Williams' family tendency to overwork without play and laughter, which further complicated problems, was mentioned, and the Williams were able to laugh at this truth about themselves. Inquiry was made as to whether Sara and Harold would like to work on their relationship with a marriage counselor. "Not now" was their decision. They would see what they could do and would call later, if necessary.

Parents and counselor exited to join the children in play. After a pleasurable ten to fifteen minutes that seemed to come to a closure (at least for the adults!), the counselor suggested that the next session be the last. It could be used for more review, as needed, and for anything else anyone had to say. She asked too that the family at that time give any impressions and feelings they have had about the counseling process, which would help the counselor in her own learning.

Some regret at ending was expressed but pleasure of change as well and some eagerness to "try it on their own" was apparent. Anne would miss playing at the office. Marie liked to come. The counselor, too, expressed some sadness about ending. The counselor suggested that they talk more about ending next time.

Session Eleven--Continuation of Review and Integration

The meeting began with some expression of fear on Harold's part that problems might recur. In that event, could they come back? The counselor reassured him that they could, and that "well family checkups" at times of family change (normal life crises, see p. 23) could be scheduled. But, foremost, she supported the tools the family now had for their own problem solving and reaffirmed her belief in their ability to deal with problem situations quite differently than previously. She gave examples observed in recent behavior to support her comment, and Harold accepted the reassurance and affirmed change.

Potential problem areas to which the family might need to be sensitive were discussed. Sara mentioned that this family had a tendency to move into acitivity when there was pain. How quickly this could happen (that tasks and household management became more important than people) was mentioned and warning signals of this were discussed. The family members were aware of this tendency and had ways of stopping its progression. The counselor mentioned the area of acting out instead of communicating directly. She asked how each of them might know when this was happening inside themselves, and how they could help themselves; how other family members could notice this tendency in another and how they could help each other. Anne related that when she felt no one in the family would pay attention to her, she ceased communicating, though she wanted to do so. Anne was helped to express her feelings if someone listened and reassured. Anne liked it more if someone played with her. Anyway, just a moment's hug helped and Anne then could work things out better for herself. That she could ask for this help was stressed and she reported, and others reaffirmed and supported, that she has changed in this way.

Other examples were mentioned, such as Sara's occasional withdrawal into a frenzy of study, and Marie's mimicking of her parents. The awareness each family member had of self and the tools that member had with which to work on his/her own stress, plus alternative behaviors the person had learned, were mentioned by the individuals and other family members commented on these tools.

Harold and Sara expressed gratitude. At the counselor's request, the family related some specific parts of the counseling process that had been helpful to them. Marie had brought a valentine and she decided to include the other children in on her idea. She went to a corner of the room and called them over, and they worked and whispered, eventually emerging to present their work. The counselor expressed her affection for the family members and said that she would miss them as well.

Future plans were discussed. Next year, after both parents had graduated, the family planned to move out of state, hopefully to a small town they had visited on vacations. The counselor expressed interest in knowing what they eventually decided. The family agreed that they would be in touch with the counselor before moving. The family inquired about the counselor's plans, and she told them of some summer travel plans she was anticipating.

No grand finale was staged to the session, though it seemed present in feeling. As the family left, Anne came to hug the counselor, followed by each of the family member's touch or hug and expression of thank you's and goodbye. Harold and Sara lingered a few minutes as the children ran into the yard toward the car. They wanted to be reassured about the possibility of couple counseling referral and were told if they decided to do this, the counselor would be glad to help them make contact with someone who could help. They again expressed their appreciation--the counselor wished them a pleasant weekend trip, and they smiled at the thought of that. Harold

offered a firm hand shake, saying they would be in touch
before they moved, and the couple left.

The counselor felt pleasure at watching the family go and
was aware that she would miss them. The counselor was aware
that they had more work to do but felt they had more tools
with which to meet their challenges.

* *

Section **5**

SOME POSSIBLE PITFALLS
IN
FAMILY COUNSELING

* *

SOME POSSIBLE PITFALLS IN FAMILY COUNSELING

Problems in counseling, like problems in families, are a part of the process of life and are considered as opportunities for growth. If a counselor does not encounter limitation in personal and professional growth he/she is wearing blinders. When one does not demand perfection of him/her self, but rather allows him/her self to use experiences for growth, the counseling profession can be rich with opportunities for learning. Some possible pitfalls in the counseling process are mentioned and with them are included suggestions for making the experience an actualizing one.

OVERLOAD OF DATA

Sometimes families present an overload of data in the beginning phase of counseling. They may give one example after another of family problem situations. Usually, any one example, throughly looked at, can reveal core problems or themes. More examples may represent repetition of themes. Too much data will not allow time for the deeper exploration necessary for effective counseling. Consequently, as themes emerge, limiting and focusing the amount of data helps to achieve an in-depth view that is necessary for unveiling the system. At any rate, the focus is always more on the process than the content.

RELUCTANCE OR EAGERNESS ON THE PART OF THE COUNSELOR

Reluctance on the part of the hesitant counselor might cause the counselor to remain at the door of Phase I or Phase II without entering either. If issues are not met head on with the family, counseling sessions may appear more like friendly chats than work periods. Direct communication, vital to unveiling the family system, would fail to occur. Taking a chance, upsetting the balance, and risking the unknown emotional discharges to make explicit the implied, are necessary behaviors of the counselor if he/she is to move into the process of counseling.

135

Most counselors report some hesitancy or self-doubt just at the point that the apex of a session is about to be reached. An effective counselor knows that he will likely feel some hesitancy and learns to recognize that experience in self. The counselor then can learn the feel of the desire to pull back at that crucial point and can better resist that urge.

On the other hand, eagerness might tempt a counselor to use an entire session for intense work toward change. Without warm-up, or a beginning phase, however, the quality of the work is markedly lowered. And, without closure time, the more highly emotional experiences of the apex phase are not well-integrated and are, therefore, not as well maintained as they would otherwise be.

A session containing almost entirely the intense qualities of Phase II will usually be followed by a session with more activities of Phase I and III and resistance to Phase II. This action is a cyclic occurrence in counseling that sometimes occurs naturally but needs to be recognized when it does, so the more relaxed session to follow is allowed. Don't push the river!

Ideally the counselor operates in a way that can be paralleled to the effective masseur. If in massaging a sore muscle, the masseur only lightly touches the skin, the painful area is unaffected. If the masseur abruptly and firmly goes deep into the affected area, the muscle only tightens more and becomes resistant, and surrounding tissue not before affected becomes involved. To relieve the soreness effectively, the masseur must work on the edge of the muscle's tension, gradually going deeper as the muscle relaxes. This will result in some pain, but it will be pain in the service of relief, as gradually the muscle relaxes and tension disappears. Likewise, the counselor must not avoid pain, but must use the feedback from the family members to work where they want change and at the level that engages the resistance and moves past it.

RESPECT AND CARING FOR THE FAMILY

If the counselor is, on the whole, unable to maintain a basic respect and caring for the people with whom working, the matter of continuing work with that family should be reconsidered. Sometimes families remind a counselor of personal problems and difficulties. A counselor may realize this in the first session or two and at that time can decide whether to work with the family and also with self simultaneously, as both approaches will be necessary. Or, at this time, the counselor may decide this personal consideration is not a positive gesture. The time alone that it takes to work with a family that challenges the edge of one's personal growth is a major issue to consider. When time or energy may not allow both foci the family may be assigned to another counselor. It is to the advantage of doing the best work that this option needs to be maintained by the counselor.

The counselor may try to move beyond personal reaction to the family with the help of supervision of personal counseling or self-help to increase self-awareness. The counselor also may bring in another counselor to aid with the family, and/or gradually transfer the case to the co-counselor. If time and situation provide, and the counselor has the motivation, working with a family with whom personal difficulty occurs can provide the counselor with opportunity for personal and professional learning, but the counselor must be prepared to invest extra time and energy for the learning.

SIDING

A counselor may find himself siding with one family member against another. When this occurs, the counselor needs to gain feeling for and understanding of each person in the family, particularly the ones toward which negative feeling exists. The counselor may be aided in gaining this by role playing that family member. Further, when siding occurs, it is a sure sign that the counselor has lost a systems view of the family. The counselor will be aided by reviewing personal system assessment and keeping a close review on each session to check his own interaction and sight the blind spots in his efforts toward becoming a non-judgmental viewer and facilitator of systems change.

RELUCTANCE OF THE FAMILY TO CHANGE

Although families want to change and may have contracted to make certain change, systems tend to gain lives of their own. They are powerful and compelling, seeking their own equilibrium. When a counselor aids a family toward agreed-upon change, frequently the family unknowingly fights the very change they want. Old patterns are more comfortable because the patterns are familiar. The unknown can seem frightening. When this tendency occurs, first check the timing to be sure that somehow the family has not been pushed to the change. The family should have moved through a process of gradual assessing and changing in a safe atmosphere and at their decision.

If the timing is too fast, a counselor needs to review the situation to find the point where the change became the

counselor's venture rather than a joint one. Then, the counselor lets own mistake be known and back-tracks. If the problem is not timing, and if the counselor is following one-half
step behind a family's lead, the counselor then may work
towards increased awareness by the family of the difficulty
of change. The counselor may become a teacher and describe
the problem of system change. Further, the counselor will
need to continue to work with the family just on the edge of
their reluctance, not pushing, nor failing to help them comfort themselves. The counselor needs patience with small
steps in growth and the ability to offer support while the
family takes risks.

FAMILY DOES NOT ENGAGE IN CHANGE

Sometimes the counselor can see the pain in families, and
wants to help more than they want the help. This desire if
acted upon consistently ends in the family's resistance. A
situation develops that can be described as, "Please let me
help you; it helps me so much." Here a counselor must recognize that one may be trying to meet personal needs at the
expense of the family, and their resistance is signaling
their reaction to this fact.

The effective counselor must always remember that a counselor is a facilitator of people doing their own changing.
If the family does not engage in a process toward change, the
counselor cannot counsel. The counselor will do better to
face the reality and explain the situation to the family as
the counselor perceives it. The counselor may inquire as to
what the family would like to do, demonstrating once again
belief in their ability to make change and willingness to
help, yet making certain that they take the lead. If they do
not, the counselor may suggest that counseling end, to resume
again should the family decide to come for assistance in
changes they want to make.

COUNSELOR TAKES A MAGIC HEALER OR JUDGE ROLE

A counselor is not a judge or jury for the family, but
often the family may want to make him into one. If a family
is operating within a rigid framework when they come to see
the counselor, it is likely they will have already decided
which of their members is wrong or which is bad, as well as
what the counseling task should be in changing that person.
True, one might receive glory and praise if one could work
magic and make changes simply by passing judgment on members
and by telling them what to do differently. But if one tries
and is not successful the consequences are costly to all. A
counselor's legitimate rewards are many, so don't try to gather
the rewards of worshipers to feed personal ego.

138

The counselor is a co-worker with the family helping them to describe their family system and to assist them in gaining tools to make their own change. If a counselor finds himself becoming the manipulator of outcomes rather than the facilitator of increased awareness and clearer communication, toward producing different outcomes, he will not be the first counselor to whom this has happened. Once a counselor becomes aware of this, the counselor should try to discuss with the family the fact that one does not like the way he/she and the family members have been working together. Likely the family members are discontent, too. A counselor might suggest that a certain way has not worked and that he/she would like to elicit agreement to try another way. A counselor may need to follow the "rule book" of a systems assessment (pp. 13-27) in a somewhat ritualistic way for a time to keep self in a systems focus. The counselor can overcome this problem also by striving to create a growth-enhancing system between self and the family members. By recording sessions and noting carefully one's listening skills, a counselor can assist self in working by following a half-step behind.

COUNSELOR BECOMES A PART OF THE DYSFUNCTIONAL SYSTEM

Sometimes a particular family system is so compelling that a counselor may find unwillingness a part of the system, acting as the other family members do in their conflict. The counselor may develop the same blind spots that the family has, share the same system, the same feeling of helplessness, the same projections, and whatever else is debilitating to the system. The counselor may help avoid or deal with this problem by video or audio taping sessions and closely examining just when and how one falls into this situation. The counselor will need to increase self awareness by looking closely at what personally is "hooked" in him/her by the system, so that when that facet of self is potentially seduced into the system again, the counselor can be aware of what is occurring and choose alternative behaviors.

COUNSELOR MUST TAKE CARE OF SELF

Families may want to call a counselor day and night. The family may want the counselor to come at hours disruptive to personal and family life. A counselor may experience so many needs in his clients that need for working never ends. Demands always exceed the time necessary to do a good job. There is no time for review and reflection. When this happens the counselor and the families are both losers. A counselor may need to select just two or three families with whom to work within the manner described in this writing, and review these

139

"The counselor may help avoid or deal
with becoming a part of the dysfunctional system by video or audio taping
sessions and closely examining just
when and how the counselor falls into
this situation."

sessions carefully for personal learning. Gradually, a counselor may be able to work with more families in a more thorough
manner, but there may always be more need than time and energy.
A counselor must remember that one's own self is the best
instrument in family counseling and can be effective only to
the degree that one nurtures and takes care of self.

Counselor may use video playback with the family
members to help analyze what occurred and the
implications.

* *

BIBLIOGRAPHY

* *

BIBLIOGRAPHY

ACKERMAN, N. W. The Psychodynamics of Family Life. New York: Basic Books, 1951.

ACKERMAN, N. W., LIEB, J. and PIERCE, J. K. (eds.) Family Therapy in Transition. New York: Little Brown, 1970.

ASSAGIOLLI, R. Psychosynthesis. A Manual of Principle and Techniques. New York: Viking Press, 1971

BELL, NORMAN W. and VOGEL, EZRA F. The Family. New York: The Free Press, 1968.

BELL, R. R. A Bibliography of American Family Problem Areas. Philadelphia: Society for the Study of Social Problems, (Temple University), 1964.

BERNE, E. The Games People Play. New York: Grove Press, 1964.

BOCH, G. R. and WYDEN, P. The Intimate Enemy: How to Fight Fair in Love and Marriage. New York: William Morrow, 1969.

BUBER, MARTIN. I and Thou. New York: Charles Scribner & Sons, 1970.

CHANCE, ERIKA. Families in Treatment. New York: Basic Books, 1959.

CHISELIN, E. (Ed.) The Creative Process. Berkeley: University of California Press, 1952.

CORSINI, R. J. Role Playing in Psychotherapy - A Manual. Chicago: Aldine Press, 1966.

ERIKSON, ERIK H. "Identity and the Life Cycle." Psychological Issues. Vol. 1, No. 1, Monograph 1. New York: International University Press, Inc., 1959.

EVANS, RICHARD I. Dialogue with Erik Erikson. New York: Harper & Row, 1967.

FEBREIRA, A. J. and WINTER, W. D. "Family Interaction and Decision Making." Archives of General Psychiatry, 1965, XIII, 214-223.

FORD, FREDERICK R. and HERRICK, JOAN M. "Family Rules." Paper presented at Southwestern Regional Meeting, American Orthopsychiatry Association, Galveston, Texas, November 1972.

FRIEDMAN, A. A. "The Incomplete Family in Family Therapy."
Family Process, February, 1963, Vol. 1. 288-301.

FRIEDMAN, A. S., BORZORMENYI-NAGY, I., JURGELS, J. E., LINCOLN,
GERALDINE, MITCHELL, H. E., SONNE, J. D., SPECK, R. V. AND
SPIVAK, G. Psychotherapy for the Whole Family. New York:
Springer Publishing Co., 1965.

FROMM, E. Escape from Freedom. New York: Holt, Rinehart &
Winston, 1941.

GIFFIN, KIM and PATTON, BOBBY R. (Eds.) Basic Readings in
Interpersonal Communication. New York: Harper & Row, 1971.

GIFFIN, KIM and PATTON, BOBBY R. Fundamentals of Interpersonal
Communication. New York: Harper & Row, 1971.

GORDON, THOMAS. Parent Effectiveness Training. New York:
P. H. Wyden, 1970.

GORDON, WILLIAM J. J. Synectics, The Development of Creative
Capacity. New York: MacMillan, 1968.

HALEY, J. Strategics of Psychotherapy. New York: Grune &
Stratton, 1963.

HALEY, J. Changing Families, A Family Therapy Reader. New
York: Grune & Stratton, Inc., 1971.

HALEY, J. and HOFFMAN, L. Techniques of Family Therapy. New
York: Basic Books, 1967.

HARDING, E. The Way of All Women. New York: C. P. Putnam,
1970.

HAYAKAWA, S. E. (Ed.) The Use and Misuse of Language. New
York: Harper & Row, 1962.

HEREFORD, C. F. Changing Parental Attitudes Through Group
Discussion. Austin, Texas: University of Texas Press, 1963.

JACKSON, D. D. "Family rules: The Marital Quid Pro Quo."
Archives of General Psychiatry, 1965, 12, 589-594.

JACKSON, D. D. (Ed.) Communication, Family and Marriage,
Human Communication, Vol. I. Palo Alto: Science & Behavior
Books, 1968.

JOURARD, S. M. The Transparent Self. Princeton, N. J.:
D. Van Nostrand Publishers, 1964.

JOURARD, S. M. Disclosing Man to Himself. Princeton, N. J.:
D. Van Nostrand Publishers, 1968.

JUNG, C. G. Contributions to Analytical Psychology. New York:
Harcourt, Brace & World, 1928.

JUNG, C. G. Modern Man in Search of a Soul. New York:
Harcourt Brace & World, 1933.

JUNG, C. G. Man and His Symbols. New York: Dell Publishing
Company, 1964

LEWIS, J. M., BEAVERS, W. R., GOSSETT, J. T., AUSTIN-PHILLIPS,
VIRGINIA. No Single Thread, Psychological Help in Family
Systems. New York: Brunner-Mazel, 1976.

MACLENNAN, B. W. and FELSENFELD, N. Group Counseling and
Psycho-Therapy with Adolescents. New York: Columbia University Press, 1968.

MASLOW, A. H. Toward a Psychology of Being. Princeton, N. J.:
D. Van Nostrand, 1962.

MASLOW, A. H. The Farther Reaches of Human Nature. New York:
Viking Press, 1971.

MORENO, J. L. Who Shall Survive? Foundations of Sociometry,
Group Psychotherapy and Sociodrama. New York: Beacon
House, 1953.

OTTO, H. A. and MANN, J. Ways of Growth: Approaches to
Expanding Awareness. New York: Viking Press, 1968.

PERLS, F., HEFFERLINE, R. F. and GOODMAN, P. Gestalt Therapy.
New York: Dell Publishing Company, 1951

ROGERS, C. R. and STEVENS, B. Person to Person: The Problems
of Being Human. Lafayette, California: Real People Press,
1967.

SAGER, CLIFFORD, J. and KAPLAN, HELEN S. (Eds.) Progress in
Group and Family Therapy. New York: Bruner-Mazel, 1972.

SATIR, VIRGINIA M. Conjoint Family Therapy: A Guide to
Theory and Technique. Palo Alto: Science & Behavior Books,
1964.

SATIR, VIRGINIA M. "The Family as a Treatment Unit." Confina
Psychiatrics, 8, 37-42, 1965.

SATIR, VIRGINIA M. Peoplemaking. Palo Alto: Science & Behavior Books, 1972.

SORENO, KENNETH K. and MORTENSEN, C. O. Foundations of Communication Theory. New York: Harper & Row, 1973.

WATZLAWICK, P. An Anthology of Human Communication. (Text and Two-Hour Tape), Palo Alto: Science & Behavior Books, 1964.

WATZLAWICK, P. "A Structured Family Interview." Family Process, February, 1966, Vol. 5, 256-271.

* *

I N D E X

* *

* *

A B O U T

T H E

A U T H O R S

* *

ABOUT THE AUTHOR

LAURA SUE DODSON, PSYCHO-
THERAPIST, CONSULTANT, AUTHOR,
TEACHER

Dr. Dodson consults with
counselors and therapists and
conducts seminars in family
therapy throughout the United
States and in Canada. She is in
private practice in Denver, Colorado. Jungian phychology and the
process of individuation, as it
relates to family systems and
family therapy, is an area of
particular interest to her.

Dr. Dodson is affiliated
with the Evergreen Consultants,
Evergreen, Colorado where she
works with individuals, couples,
and families. She has taught couple and family therapy in
classes in various locations such as the Dallas Family Guid-
ance Clinic and Evergreen Development Center. She also lec-
tures in Jungian Psychology.

Co-founder and co-director of the Evergreen Institute, a
non-profit, educationally incorporated center for teaching
professionals various therapies and for conducting workshops of
a psychological-educational nature with individuals, couples,
and families was a major interest during 1966-1973.

DR. DODSON CURRENTLY IS ACTIVE AS A PSYCHOTHERAPIST IN
PRIVATE PRACTICE, CONSULTANT, AND TEACHER IN FAMILY THERAPY
AND COUPLE THERAPY.

Date Due

ABOUT THE EDITOR

DeWayne J. Kurpius has just completed an extensive three-phase research and development project during which time he and Sue Dodson collaborated as conceptualizers, trainers, and program developers. One of their programs, national in scope, provided renewal training seminars in "Counseling the Family as a Group" for university counselor education professors. Dr. Kurpius also has published materials which define systematic training approaches for entry level trainees, as well as advanced graduate students in both teacher education and counselor education. He is currently co-authoring three new books to be published in 1977. They will focus on influencing the school learning environment, supervision of applied training, and psychoeducational consultation.

As a consultant, Dr. Kurpius has worked with a wide variety of situations and organizations such as mental health clinics, universities, medical schools, public schools, state departments of public instruction and the U.S. Office of Education.

Dr. Kurpius currently is teaching and conducting research in the areas of counselor training and consultation. His present research thrust is directed toward explicating the interaction variables which influence human and organizational change.

DeWayne J. Kurpius is an associate professor of education at Indiana University.